THE BONUS YEARS

a postscript to *Drawn by the Light*

by Arthur O. Roberts

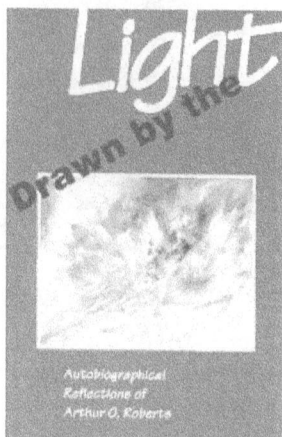

Light

Drawn by the

Autobiographical
Reflections of
Arthur O. Roberts

Arthur O. Roberts knows well the person that lives inside his skin. In his autobiographical reflections— *Drawn by the Light*—he reveals a journey filled with experiences both divine and painfully human. Each chapter tells with insight and candor the first-person story of a specific span of time in the author's life. An overview written in third person introduces each of these chapters. The years since 1993 when *Drawn by the Light* was published are identified as *The Bonus Years*.

THE
BONUS
YEARS

a postscript to

Drawn by the Light
autobiographical reflections
of Arthur O. Roberts

B

BARCLAY PRESS
NEWBERG, OREGON

THE BONUS YEARS
a postscript to *Drawn by the Light*

Published by Barclay Press, Newberg, Oregon
www.barclaypress.com

Printed in the United States of America

ISBN 978-1-59498-033-6

Contents

vii – Foreword

1 – The Inward Journey

5 – About Our Family

7 – Health Issues

8 – The Political Years

17 – Public Ministry

22 – Travel

25 – Enjoying Life in a Coastal Village

29 – Enjoying Life in a Retirement Community

43 – Reflections

45 – Passing On a Legacy

54 – Recent Poetry and Prose
(listed on next page)

131 – Addendum

Transitions (Momentous or Otherwise) over Sixty Years \ 131

Events of Varying Importance in the Roberts'
First Sixty Years of Marriage (1943-2003) \ 133

Articles, Lectures, Chapters, Honors,
and Special Assignments \ 140

Publications \ 143

Pastoral and Academic Ministry \ 144

Poems

11 – Sonnet on Local Governance

41 – Puttering Around

51 – With Mystical Power

55 – Prayer for President Obama

56 – Benedictory Prayer

57 – "Right for You"

58 – A Cheerful Red

59 – O, Yes, It's Ray

60 – The Eighth D-mension

62 – God's Lifting Power

63 – That Old Fir Tree

64 – To the Green Hills

64 – Tribute to Mackey Hill

65 – Tribute to Fred and Mardella Newkirk

66 – "Truth Has Prospered"

67 – "I Like Being Ten!"

68 – Cheers

68 – To Trask

69 – To Laura and James

70 – To April and Eric

71 – Far and Near

72 – Glorious Joy

73 – Advent

74 – Panic Attack

75 – A Birthday

76 – Golden Years

77 – Birthday

113 – Fair Skies

114 – Foliage Isn't Everything

116 – "Lord Save Me!"

Prose

53 – Yes, Lord!

78 – ABC's of Theology

84 – Controlling Auditory Space in the Classroom

86 – Pleasant Ridge Grade School Valedictory

87 – George Fox University Commencement 2011

91 – Trouble and Triumph in Anthropolis

102 – Visions and Dreams

107 – Finding Joy

113 – Stormy Weather

117 – How the Kingdom of God Flourishes

122 – Weeds

127 – Pondering Paradigm Shifts in Certain Biblical Models

129 – Christmas 2011

Foreword

Reading *The Bonus Years* by seasoned author Arthur O. Roberts brings to mind the masterful essays that Samuel Johnson wrote in the early 1750s, which have come down to us today as the book *The Rambler*. Indeed, Arthur's writings here are "exquisite ramblings" spanning a lifetime of faithful living.

In *The Rambler* Johnson reminds us that the task of an author is "either to teach what is not known, or to recommend known truths by his manner of adorning them; either to let new light in upon the mind, and open new scenes to the prospect, or to vary the dress and situation of common objects, so as to give them fresh grace and more powerful attractions, to spread such flowers over the regions through which the intellect has already made its progress, as may tempt it to return, and take a second view of things hastily passed over, or negligently regarded" (*The Rambler*, Tuesday, March 27, 1750).

Arthur Roberts does all of this and more. *The Bonus Years* is a cornucopia of distilled wisdom. He ambles over a host of subjects from political engagement to Quaker witness to playing Scrabble to public ministry to automobile ownership to retirement living. The subject matter is confined only by the imagination of the author, and Arthur's imagination is expansive indeed.

In the hands of a lesser writer this could easily result in simply a jumble of ideas and thoughts and observations. But Arthur is most assuredly not a "lesser writer." Somehow, I do not exactly know how, he is able to weave into an organic whole stories and poems and essays on a vast array of topics, carefully adding astute observations on the most common ventures of life.

The Bonus Years is a joy to read. Arthur's poems charm the heart, his essays instruct the mind, and his insights enlarge the soul.

I urge you to read *The Bonus Years* slowly, quietly, prayerfully. Linger on the delightful word choice. Savor the carefully crafted poems. Read it again and again. It will not disappoint.

—*Richard J. Foster*

I have learned that maturity
has more to do with what types
of experiences you have had and
what you have learned from them
and less to do with how many
birthdays you've celebrated.

—Gusten Lutter, Jr.

The Inward Journey

The Lord graciously granted bonus years to Arthur and Fern Roberts, beyond the threshold three score and ten. During this time their spiritual journey achieved greater intimacy with God, closer bonding with each other, heightened rapport with adult children and their families, and a greater love for fellow trekkers along life's trail. Nudged by the Holy Spirit, Fern sometimes took a lead in Bible and devotional reading during regular morning worship and prayer time together. This brought a listening, healing silence to Arthur, helpful after decades of professorial ministry to others through the spoken and written word. Together they rejoiced in grandchildren (no longer little folks frolicking on the beach!). They shared the excitement and struggles as these young people matured and found appropriate spheres of work, friendship, marriage, and as they began rearing children of their own. The Lord urged the grandparents to pray daily for these grandchildren, sometimes prompting them to send letters of admonition, counsel, or concern. In due course great-grandchildren warmed the hearts of this old couple, too, and let them rejoice in the wonder and beauty of the ongoing generations of human life.

During bonus years the Spirit bound together the hearts of this couple more firmly than ever as they celebrated life together, first fifty years, then sixty, sixty-five, sixty-eight, sixty-nine, seventy.

Their retirement home at Yachats by the sea afforded heightened appreciation for the Creator, who ministered to them through cresting waves, spouting whales, friendly crows, and soaring seagulls; through shoreline walks, glorious sunsets, the symmetry of rippled sand, and agates waiting patiently to be polished. Thus their senses more fully became God's messengers. In this village the Lord heightened the Quaker couple's appreciation for the larger body of Christ, directing them to share in a local Presbyterian church, and to participate in city affairs. Thus the Lord gave them increased appreciation for persons outside familiar circles of acquaintance and their cherished Quaker covenant fellowship.

The Holy Spirit continued to teach them how to show love to each other, to be more considerate and sensitive to friends and neighbors. During these golden years they became friends and resources to younger persons beyond their family circle, first in the village of Yachats, and then in the Newberg and George Fox communities when in their eighties they moved back to the place where they had lived and labored so long. The Holy Spirit nudged the couple to continue to serve others, now more diligently because they were released from full-time jobs. "You aren't on the shelf," insisted the Spirit, "under my anointing use your gifts for a wider audience." And so they did. Fern intensified her quilt making, gifting and blessing young parents taking babies home from birthing rooms. Renewed interaction with collegians—some born after they had retired— revitalized jaded spirits. Mentoring graduate students became a ministry for Arthur, who helped young scholars comprehend and articulate truth more clearly. He now had time to write. He produced several books of prose and poetry, as well as numerous articles and sermons.

The Spirit prompted them in various ways to share accumulated material wealth, not just helping grandkids buy cars or pay for schooling, but also supporting church and charitable ministries. As a result of prudent living, debt avoidance, and careful investments, the Lord entrusted them with sufficient financial resources to live comfortably in retirement and still contribute to needs of others—going well beyond a lifelong practice of tithing income.

Loss of acute hearing released them more closely to observe visually and to relish the beauty of natural things. The Creator helped them see glory in undulating cloud formations, petals of a flower, the mountains to the north, fields of ripening grain, the red and golden fall foliage, and the graceful flight of soaring birds. Fern became a tutor in this transition, helping her bookish mate more attentively to read and revel in God's other book, nature, more fully to encompass the aesthetic within the holy.

They discovered that getting old isn't easy. But the Lord walked with them through physical pain and illness, through embarrassing episodes of forgetting names, through diminishing physical strength and agility. The Lord helped them face death of friends and loved ones, to cope with the wail of ambulances arriving at their retirement center, and to cope with posted death notices. (The words of the poet John Donne pealed ominously: "ask not for whom the bell tolls...!") Under these stresses the Spirit became, indeed, the Comforter—empowering them to overcome anxieties, resist depression, accept and reciprocate love more easily, and to strengthen trust.

The Lord gathered them to Himself—and to each other—more closely as bodily strength waned, when sickness laid them low, during gloomy winter days, but also in bright and long summer days! Fern's love and the hand of the Spirit led Arthur through chasms of intellectual doubt, when the confident author of *Exploring Heaven* was assailed by academic atheists preaching "liberation" from religion. But Truth prevailed against Satan, the "father of lies," and brought peace of mind—and joy—to the old scholar, and to his loving wife. Thus the Spirit renewed their confidence in Jesus' resurrection promise of a heavenly home, and gave them peace in body, mind, and spirit.

About Our Family

During the early Yachats years, our daughters also resided at the coast. Trish lived in nearby Waldport and served as church secretary for the Yachats Community Presbyterian Church. This meant her daughters April and Laura were often at our home, enjoying the beach, and active in school and church activities. Our other daughter Teri, with husband John, lived for several years up the coast at Neskowin teaching in area schools. This meant we could see them frequently; we could watch Heidi play volleyball and John David wrestle—and share our beach and love with them. When they moved to Arizona, and subsequently to California, we saw them less frequently. Our son, Lloyd, and his wife Cheryl had settled in a hilltop home above The Dalles. He had been a mill foreman for many years, then got into other things, including overseer of cherry harvesting. We enjoyed occasional visits with Seth, Sarah, and Heather. Lloyd's daughter Robin had lived mostly with her mother, Barbara Collins, in nearby Dundee, but as a young adult lived and worked in the Portland area, visiting us often.

During these bonus years, our grandchildren's affinity circles gradually widened outside family and became filled with friends and associates, their days crowded with jobs and social activities. As for careers, Robin graduated from Oregon State University and has held various positions as business consultant and teacher. Sarah graduated from George Fox University in business administration and has held jobs in that field. April graduated from Lewis and Clark College and after a few years found herself in Maryland working for a government agency. Heidi graduated from Lewis and Clark also, but added a teaching credential from George Fox University, and has been teaching in coastal communities. Laura graduated from Linfield College and took graduate work at Pacific

University to become an optometrist. Seth chose a non-academic route and works as a skilled craftsman. Heather took college classes and has worked as a teaching aide. John David has taken various college courses and became a yoga instructor.

As adults now, our grandchildren—as well as our children—have their own stories to tell, in due time, about their journeys through life, about hard times and good times, about love and marriage, adventures at home and abroad, children and jobs, and also sorrows and joys. They have experienced ups and downs, as all of us have, with failures and successes. Our emotions cycle in sync with theirs. Yes, we became increasingly peripheral to their lives; but even as we "wait in the wings" we know they love us. We support them daily by prayer. We feel particularly blessed when they initiate phone calls, correspondence, or visits. We are confident that in their own manner they will demonstrate, and perhaps narrate, how in redemptive grace God has extended hands of love to them, helping them to live faithfully in the community of Christ. We pray this will be so. And now we are blessed with great-grandchildren: Heather's son, Zain; Robin and Michael's children, Quinn and Mia Jade; Sarah and Luke's son, Aiden; Heidi and Sean's sons, John Trask and Rigel Wilson; and April and Eric's sons Gabriel Joseph and Evander Maurice. We welcome these little ones (twenty-first century people) into the extended family circle, and pray for them, too.

As our children approached or reached retirement age, family bonding became stronger. We could communicate via phone or internet more often. They had time and resources for more visits. We appreciated letters, phone calls, and personal contacts with my brother Warren in Idaho until his death in 2013; with various nieces and nephews (children of Warren and of previously deceased sisters Lucille and Marjorie); and with Fern's cousins Doris Aschim and Vernon Maxson.

Health Issues

With a few exceptions our health was good during early bonus years. Fern had a hip replacement and I prostate surgery during the Yachats chapter of our lives. I was diagnosed with gastrointestinal disease (GERD), and remain on medication and lifestyle disciplines to control it. I had a bout with atrial fibrillation (probably induced by noxious fumes from paint remover). In 2003 Fern fell prey to a virulent bug, *clostridium difficile*, and was hospitalized in Newport for eleven days. It was life threatening. Thankfully the drug Vancomycin beat down

> *The only bank where you can deposit all your savings is your memory. That bank will never go bankrupt.*
>
> — Yevtushenko, Yevgeny
> *Wild Berries (Holt, 1984) p. 57*

the bug. This illness signaled it was time to enter Friendsview Retirement Community, and when a new building was constructed—Creekside—we moved into a third floor apartment, December 1, 2003. Fern suffered a second episode of this bug soon after we moved, and again was hospitalized. Fortunately, there has been no recurrence.

Our Yachats property proceeds were divided four ways. We used a portion to buy into Friendsview, then divided the rest: Teri's share to help her and John purchase that coast house for a rental—and possible retirement home, Trish's to reduce property debt, and Lloyd's to secure monthly income from an annuity.

7

The Political Years

One pleasant evening in Yachats, Fern and I decided to attend a council meeting. We had recently retired to this Oregon coastal village, and it seemed a good opportunity to learn about issues facing our community. The visit revived interest in things political. When an opening came I ran for a council seat and upon winning served a four-year term, from 1989-93. A couple years later I was appointed to fill a vacancy. One major contribution as a councilor was to help negotiate purchase (for $190,000) of no longer needed property from the Lincoln County School District. The building and grounds—dubbed "The Commons"—has since served as City Hall, recreational area, and youth center.

In 1996 I ran for the office of mayor. For how this came about I draw upon a privately published account of a major controversy that engulfed our pleasant town, *The Story of CR 804 South*. One autumn day in 1996, the sole candidate for mayor on the November ballot backed out. Telephone technician Larry Nixon averred he had endured too many hassles by a few area residents about alleged (but unproven) conflicts of interest. His professional work, he said, sufficed to keep him busy without piling on additional hours of demanding volunteer service for hometown neighbors. (He had already served on the council for several years, and would do so again in future years.) It was too late to remove Nixon's name from the ballot, or to add new ones, so concerned citizens cast about for write-in candidates. One approached me at the post office and asked if I would stand for mayor. "Well," I responded, "you can write in my name if you wish." Being prodded to publicize this on-the-spot decision, my friends and I put up a few signs and passed the word around to neighbors.

The prospects of Roberts becoming mayor, however, alarmed the folks who had needled Nixon to withdraw! So promptly they secured and promoted an *alternate* write-in candidate, one more amenable to their agenda, Howard Osborn. A modest and friendly campaign ensued in the remaining few weeks prior to election. I won the election by *one* vote, a decision confirmed after mandatory re-tabulation! When this was announced at the next council meeting, Osborn graciously conceded victory; but a few days later he told the victor, "my people want me to appeal." And appeal they did, claiming that alternate first names for Osborn, had they been counted, would have given him the victory. They claimed "Harry" and "Harold" are misspellings for Howard, and that election law allows for tallying misspellings as well as initials. The county and the State Department of Elections, however, affirmed the legal correctness of the tally. So did the Oregon Court of Appeals, on grounds that persons tallying write-in votes would have no way accurately to know whether variant given names for a common first name refer to the same or another person, and therefore *must not engage in guessing*. The burden of proof for write-in elections lies upon voters being knowledgeable about candidates, announced the court. I took office a few days after the January verdict.

Why all this fuss and legal challenge about an election of a volunteer mayor in a small coastal town whose major industries are tourism and retirement? Here's the reason. Those whom Osborn dubbed "my people" turned out to be a coterie of folks wanting to reclaim for public use an old (1890s) sixty-foot right of way through a number of shoreline homes, including that of the newly-elected mayor! In the fall of 1996, during a hearing on a requested lot division in the area, three Yachats area persons had "discovered" from county records that this old right of way had never been vacated *formally*.

Knowing that action by Lincoln County to vacate this over-platted right of way would require concurrence by the city of Yachats, these persons, grouped within a local "Friends of the CR 804" and a regional organization, "Oregon Shores Coastal Coalition," wanted a mayor favorable to their position. I had been ignorant of this, but soon became very much aware of it, for an extended, costly, and emotionally draining struggle over the issue commenced shortly after I took office and continued beyond my four years of service.

Before summarizing this controversy I should note some more pleasant aspects of the two terms I served as mayor. At the first council session, faithful to my ancestral Quaker testimony against swearing oaths—more costly to them than to me—I requested and was privileged to accept the office by solemn affirmation. Interestingly, other new councilors did, too, and for some years, at least, this practice became the norm!

As a councilor I had edited a monthly newsletter, a task subsequently assumed by the city recorder. In pondering how to adapt editorial skills to council meetings I decided to write a poem for each month, read it at the beginning of the session, and include it in the monthly newsletter along with the water bill. I did this each month of the four years. Upon concluding my mayoral leadership these poems were published by the city (at no cost to them) in cooperation with Barclay Press—*Let the Spirit Soar*. The first month's poem, a sonnet, appears on the following page.

At my first meeting I was bothered by a lack of order through citizen interruptions. I even had to gavel down one vociferous fellow and recess that meeting to cool things down. Rough start! Things had to change. Several years earlier, when I served on council, I had found a parliamentary system more congenial to ordinary citizens. Briefly put, the Keesey system calls for consensus on procedural matters, with voting reserved for policy issues. No more wrangling over amendments. Council deliberates until a clear motion is agreed to, then it is discussed fully, and voted up or down. Not quite at the level of a Quaker meeting for business but a reasonable secular approximation. So, as mayor I followed this system consistently. We also defined more clearly our governance model. Oregon towns are not chartered like New England town meet-

Sonnet on Local Governance

Governance is not much fun
when people bicker and complain,
when sewers flood from too much rain.
It seems you can't please everyone.
But when all is said and done
troubles wax but also wane.
Civility and truth sustain
eras of good will. For one
whose joy it is to serve another
by making order out of social
clutter, duty to a neighbor
really is a rather special
    sort of civic love,
    kindled from Above.

(January 1997)

ings (although some folks had acted as if they were). We arranged set agenda times for public input, not only on state mandated matters such as land use, but also for other citizen concerns. These changes made city politics and governance more civil.

As a public official I became very much aware of the importance of water to a community. Two issues arose for which I gave direction. One winter a storm took out the weir that provided a holding pond for water to homes and businesses. It was located on federal land. So we faced a bureaucracy that moved slowly and was pressured by folks who don't want the forest tampered with. We solved this problem by preserving our water right but building our own storage tank downstream on city property and piping the water there from the stream source, and from there on down to the central distribution facility. We also reasserted our water right to the Yachats River should our two creeks ever prove insufficient.

A second issue offered an ethical tangle. Upon incorporation the city had accepted a water source south of its border, and piped all service from a central holding facility in town. The eight owners were assured of water at a monthly cost proportionate to what city citizens pay in monthly fees and taxes. Well, the south source soon dried up. Decades later the old pipe, overlaid by coastal Highway 101, rusted out. What to do? By law a city is not required to provide utilities beyond its borders. There was no written agreement, only reliable testimony from old timers about a covenant sealed by a handshake. To tear up the winding coast highway for two or three miles would cost several hundred thousand dollars, maybe millions. I held meetings with affected owners—few but affluent, some poised for lawsuits—and affirmed our faith that a fair solution could be found. So I asked our public works director, Rod Carrasco, to research a technical solution. He did, and came up with this plan: thread a flexible three-inch pipe down the old metal four-inch one, cutting in for joints only in a few places as needed. It worked! For forty thousand dollars we solved the problem for the few and for the many, and did so with ethical integrity. This win-win solution blessed this old professor of ethics!

And now, back to the most difficult issue of all, County Road 804 South. Here's the story, with particular emphasis upon properties fronting the ocean, those coveted for return to public use. In 1953 Lincoln County commissioners had approved Ocean Crest Subdivision in a part of Yachats, *including its roadways*. The subdivision created thirty lots over a portion of an old "Waldport to Yahutes" easement, authorized in the 1890s but *never built upon nor improved as surveyed*. One lot was dedicated for public beach access. Another is

12

owned by the city and dedicated as an overlook area. Twenty-five homes had been built in the subdivision. The commissioners believed that in approving the subdivision they had legally terminated the easement. A road to replace the old right of way was designated and built. The new road, Ocean View Drive, runs just inland roughly parallel to the old survey. County maps were changed to show the new road, new lots, and new property owners. The city-named Ocean View Drive then appeared on county records as CR 804. No deeds showed any remnant loops of the old easement. The county began taxing new property owners for their lots as deeded.

Although Lincoln County *believed* it had vacated 804 South, by today's standards either it was not done properly or not recorded appropriately. Persons opposing vacation wanted the sixty-foot-wide easement to revert to the public, at whatever cost to the property owners or their heirs—whom zealots likened to recipients of stolen goods. Busily they lobbied county and state officials and solicited public sympathy to their cause, linking it to an earlier successful effort to validate a public right of way along the bluff *north* of town. Outraged homeowners insisted that 804 North and 804 South were very different situations. 804 North had been in continuous use, first as an access road and then as a pedestrian path, with easements shown on deeds.

In December 1996 affected owners met to ponder options. Then they asked Lincoln County Commissioners to take whatever action was needed to clear titles. The county decided a petition by property owners was the appropriate way to proceed. This took months to complete by a legal firm hired by title companies. Citizens busily researched the issue to defend their rights. In that same year the city of Yachats developed its Village Circulation Plan, which turned contentious when efforts were made to insert into the document statements supporting a "bluff" trail route, obviously anticipating a city hearing on the South 804 issue. After negotiating differences with the Department of Land Conservation and Development, the city approved a plan for pedestrian and bike paths through the city, *along Ocean View Drive,* and connecting with Smelt Sands State Park and its hiking trail north of town. The plan was approved by the city and acknowledged by the state. Any edge of bluff route was deemed neither ecologically friendly nor financially feasible. At our invitation in 1997, Oregon State Parks and Recreation Department surveyed the area and agreed: a trail would not be feasible to build nor to maintain. (This proved to be *significant* testimony). Proponents of vacation gave evidence that sixty percent of Yachats shoreline is open to the public, the highest of any coastal city in Oregon.

The county commissioners held hearings, listened to and received *extensive* written testimony. And they ordered a new survey. It showed the old right of way not only transecting our subdivision but also homes and businesses along the bay—and in places over the ocean! So in 1998, firmly convinced their action was right, commissioners, with concurrence by the city of Yachats, vacated the old right of way—County Road 804 South.

Alas, this didn't end the matter. A strong Oregon land use lobby, 1000 Friends of Oregon, agreed to provide legal aid for its area advocacy arm, OSCC (Oregon Shores Conservation Coalition), despite earlier statements to the contrary; and it returned donations from outraged local members who resigned in protest. Opponents appealed through the courts, a lengthy process. In the meantime a burned-out home could not be rebuilt, pending home sales were lost, and stressed-out citizens were hospitalized. The issue was eventually remanded back to the county by the Oregon Supreme Court. At issue were requirements within both county and city charters requiring them to conform to state mandated ocean access

14

standards. We tried legislation. County attorneys and I worked with legislators to craft a bill that would essentially "grandfather in" such old over-platting actions. The bill passed House and Senate. But Governor Kitzhaber vetoed it, offering to fund mediation service instead. This course didn't seem feasible to owners until we learned of an exemption clause tucked into Oregon Department of Land Conservation and Development policy documents. It fit our case! Both county and city seized upon this "out" and soon passed actions approving it. With another years-long bout of appeals in prospect, however, it seemed prudent to accept mediation, with the exceptions process as a viable fall-back option.

The first state-appointed mediator quit, alleging the situation "not ripe." The second one, Carie Fox of Portland, Oregon, a Quaker (at least by heritage), in November of 2000 very capably conducted sessions from which came a settlement approved by all sides. In 2001 CR 804 South was officially vacated, titles cleared. Having to rescind the "Exceptions" actions as a condition for settlement, however, left that option untested as a precedent for other Oregon communities facing claims upon remnant road loops. The settlement required funding (about $250,000) from county, title companies, state, and city to provide a graveled trail *within* the Ocean View Drive roadway (completed in 2004), improve public access lots, and purchase property to connect with the trail north of town. It was a victory for the property owners, but a costly one in time, energy, and financial resources. One of my final actions on this issue consisted of nagging (by letter and by phone) one title company that had reneged on support, until they came through and reimbursed their insured owners for legal fees incurred.

In the years following this controversy, I pondered to what extent I demonstrated Christian virtue. As I see it, virtue means integrity in respect to truth as well as interpersonal relationships. The summons to justice and mercy were personally compelling. In my experience these two virtues are not easily blended in political affairs. But they *are* linked. Just political decisions to correct past errors *do* extend mercy to persons ensnared by such situations. I often brought the situation to God in prayer, and was corrected, encouraged, and calmed by the Spirit. As a writer gifted in using words, I may have overburdened officials with too many of them!

Two metaphors for faithful gospel witness are light and leaven. They depict Jesus' call to truth and his command to love. Did I focus or obscure the light of God's truth about justice and equity? The pursuit of truth involves a divine summons to reason. As Kahlil Gibran wrote: "Knowledge without reason is like a house unguarded. And even Love, Justice, and Goodness avail little if Reason be not there too" (*Secrets of the Heart*, Hallmark, 1968 p. 35).

Did I help or hinder the permeation of love through respect for opponents as well as for active concern for imperiled neighbors? In my pages and pages of argument I probably did better in focusing the light of truth on the situation than in demonstrating the leaven of love! Personal interest and public service were comingled, however, hopefully with integrity, in my mayoral years and in my efforts for justice. A few weeks before we moved back to Newberg, the Yachats city council presented Fern and me with a plaque, appointing us "ambassadors of love."

In conclusion I affirm two things. First, as followers of Jesus we are summoned to be faithful to God in *present, real-life* (even confrontational) *circumstances*, in action as well as in thought and word. Second, through traumatic struggle we can experience God's grace to steady us, to affirm us, to forgive us, to correct us, to instruct us, and to restore us to wholeness—body, mind, and spirit. I am grateful to God for this wondrous, redeeming, and sustaining grace!

Public ministry

Not having a schedule of classroom teaching during these bonus years, I was able to devote considerable time and intellectual energy to writing projects and to speaking engagements—mostly as guest minister. (Being mayor didn't take all my time and creativity, and retirement at Friendsview left us with lots of free time.) I discerned a cloud of challenges to the Christian faith and through the written and spoken word sought to provide a strong witness within a culture increasingly darkened by neo-paganism and by academic skepticism—even militant atheism. During the final decade of the century, I edited *Quaker Religious Thought,* and wrote articles for this journal, namely, "Quakers and the Broader Christian Movement," and "Quaker Understanding of Christ."

> *Language is not so much the dress as the incarnation of the thought. The word is truth become flesh. Language is the body of the idea, and it is only in the body that we can become aware of it.*
>
> *—Henry Zylstra, Testament of Vision (Eerdmans, 1958, 1965 edition) p. 60*

In 2002 Swarthmore College, in Philadelphia, sponsored a conference to honor the 350th anniversary of the Quaker movement. I presented a paper entitled "Come In at the Door! How Foxian Metaphors of Salvation Speak to Evangelical Friends." With other conference papers it was published in 2006 by the Friends Historical Association in a book entitled *George Fox's Legacy.* I wrote chapters and introductions for several other books. In 2004 I gave the plenary address before the Friends Association of Higher Education, in which I laid out the "seven pillars" of truth to support Christian education and successfully challenge the pervasive influence of secularism. These pillars are: God is sovereign, creation is good, truth is revealed, intelligence is embodied, humanity is of one blood, God's kingdom defines community, and Christ is God's redemptive Word (Published in *Quaker Religious Thought*, #102, 2005). (See pages 140-143 for a complete listing of publications.)

For twelve years I wrote "Roberts' Reflections," a monthly Internet column for Northwest Friends pastors. During these decades I preached several dozen sermons. Some are included in the book, *Sacred Ordinary*. During these bonus years I wrote thirteen books (fourteen counting this one) and the script for one cantata. (See addendum starting on page 131.)

A reward for writing is the grateful response one occasionally gets. The book *Exploring Heaven* (printed and promoted by a major publisher) elicited wide reader response. Once a pastor of a large (2000 member) Episcopal congregation in Kentucky contacted me. It was Lenten season. My book had strengthened his faith in Jesus' physical resurrection. No longer would his sermons treat Easter as just a symbol for spiritual renewal, but would herald its full force of meaning, including personally conscious eternal life in a restored cosmos. Well, this pastor arranged to visit us in Yachats, to convey gratitude and to seek guidance on a book he decided to write on the "treasures in heaven." Another reader responded to my statement that black holes might just be God's recycling center for the creation of new worlds, with a terse exclamation, "I love it!" A Midwest reader found reassurance—against a tide of literature expounding strictly symbolic meanings, or discounting the resurrection altogether—that a real heaven makes sense. We had pages of email correspondence. The book restored hope to another that heaven won't be boring. One reviewer found skepticism being supplanted by wonder and delight. Another wrote that reading the book "is like eating good Belgian chocolate," a feeling similar to that experienced when reading C. S. Lewis! A dear friend and former colleague at George Fox University found it comforting and assuring in the face of terminal cancer. I appreciated endorsements by some leading scientists and theologians, and am grateful that my book has helped restore to Christian theology a harmony between doctrines of creation and redemption. For too long, in a sort of tacit truce, the sphere of reality had been split: science gets physical stuff, religion gets spiritual stuff. It didn't work, as increasingly the social sciences claimed intangibles, too, in effect reducing religion to a subset of sociology or to mythic fiction. Churches struggled to sustain clear and convincing apologetics to match emphases upon fellowship and loving service.

> *For He [God], in truth, has given us all our senses for our pleasure; yet reserved to Himself their use as medium and avenue for His larger purposes to play upon our minds.*
>
> *Thomas Mann, Joseph in Egypt (Knopf, 1938) p. 152*

My poems in the companion book, *Prayers at Twilight*, served at a more intuitive level, helping folks cope with loss of loved ones.

In a different way I believe the book about sensuous spirituality, *Messengers of God*, has elicited an equally significant response, particularly as it has contributed to a reuniting of science and religion—the book of nature with the book of Scripture. (Granddaughter Robin wrote the scientific data about each of the five senses.) The title comes from a phrase used early in the Christian era by the philosopher Augustine. Our book was used several years after 1996 as an auxiliary text at George Fox University in the course Human Anatomy and Physiology. Most students in this course are preparing for service in health professions. I visited the class sections for several years (a hundred students in 2010) and am grateful for student interaction, mostly verbal but some tactile—friendly hugs. I treasure this note, "It is very enlightening and has encouraged me to enjoy God's creation on every level, using every sense he has blessed me with!"

At the request of Barclay Press, I updated my 1959 book, *Through Flaming Sword,* for a fifty-year anniversary edition. Readers observed that this book clarified what the seventeenth-century Quaker awakening signified, and how we might restore integrity to our Christian witness as Friends in today's world. One correspondent, an editor of an area British newspaper, after reading it began attending a Quaker meeting and became a member. He remarked that the Lord works in mysterious ways—apparently feeling it ironic that it took an Oregon author to convey the Quaker message to a Brit living in George Fox country.

During these bonus years I lectured occasionally at George Fox University and taught a few seminars on Quaker spirituality on campus and in area churches. One of my students in an ethics class I had taught in 1991, Corey Beals, engaged me in correspondence throughout his graduate education, and under a clear sense of divine direction, with which I concurred, said "yes" to an invitation to teach philosophy at his alma mater. In 2003, he moved west from an East Coast academic sojourn with wife Jill and young family, just as I had sojourned from New Hampshire fifty years earlier with Fern and our young children. I also mentored several students, some informally. One youth, eager to learn, was Chase Willcuts, a great-grandnephew of my old buddy, Jack Willcuts. As a high school student, aspiring to write, he approached me for help. I critiqued his essays and discussed with him the larger issue of life. He came often to visit us over the next several years during his college career at George Fox. Other mentees were adults. These included Presbyterian,

Evangelical Church, and Quaker ministers—and a few independent scholars—in doctoral studies in Birmingham, England, and at Fuller Seminary and George Fox Evangelical Seminary in the United States. I also maintained academic correspondence with scholars in America and in other countries, including Britain, Norway, Russia, and Australia.

In 2009 I entered an essay contest sponsored by a British journal. I didn't win, but at least my views on how to bring spiritual renewal to this nation's dwindling Quaker community of faith got some public exposure along with a hundred other entries dealing with the same theme. The contest was inspired by one that had occurred 150 years previously that had resulted in an evocative winning essay by John Rowntree, "Inquiry into the Causes of Its Decline in England and Ireland." Well, this 2009 non-Brit essay reviewed the centuries of Quaker history and noted how the drift away from Christian teachings basic to the early movement contributed to decline in the recent decades. My essay urged repentance and prayer as first steps toward renewal followed by commitment to restore a firm Christian foundation for beliefs and practices.

Travel

In 1996 Fern and I took a trip to New England. From Portland, Maine, with rented car we drove to Freeport to visit the L.L. Bean store. We bought some clothes from them, so it was fun. We drove old Hwy. 1 along the Maine coast and north to Bangor, where we stayed overnight, then meandered along the coast, then inland around Mount Washington enjoying the fall colors, wending our way through Vermont, and then into New Hampshire to visit our home and dual place of ministry during doctoral studies.

Goffstown had grown since we left the area sixty years ago. We were disappointed to find the Methodist church looking shabby. It had been converted into a second-hand clothing store when the congregation merged with the Grasmere congregation a few years previously. So we drove on to Grasmere to find, to our delight, that the Grasmere facilities (now called Hillside United Methodist) were well maintained. The pastor took us into the parsonage, remodeled since we lived there. We took pictures and reflected on our experiences there. We saw where the playpen for Teri and Trish stood, and the upstairs window from which Lloyd once nearly fell.

Sunday we drove to the Dover meetinghouse, built in 1768. It's where ancestral Roberts worshiped. My grandfather, Levi, was a member, although the family lived in New Durham nearby. Levi left in 1857 for Iowa, where he met and married Mary Bevan. (John Greenleaf Whittier's parents were married here.) Meeting for worship September 29, 1996, was at 10:30. After fifteen minutes—mostly silence save an exhortation to young disciples—children and teachers went downstairs where we could hear them singing. From the silence I and one other person shared in worship. Friends were courteous. One woman said she shared Roberts' ancestry. Afterwards we went through the large Pine Hill cemetery, finding quite a few Roberts markers. On Monday we contacted Ed and Shirley Leslie, who had agreed to help with genealogical research. From nearby Rochester they led us to the Meaderboro Friends cemetery. There we found markers for Thomas and Elizabeth (Meader) Roberts—my great-grandparents. We took pictures and rubbings of the stones. Grateful for their help, we took leave of the Leslies and drove sixty miles to Portland, Maine, took a motel, and caught the early morning flight home.

Though the flight home was uneventful—Portland to Chicago to Denver to Eugene—in Eugene my pride was deflated a bit. It seems I had left the car door ajar (shut on the seat belt) and the battery had run down. Fortunately the AAA service took care of it within half an hour and we were home at Yachats by 4 p.m.

All of nature is a shattered
mirror of divine beauty, still full
of light, but riven by darkness....
We learn in Christ the nature
of our first estate, and the divine
destiny to which we are called,
we begin to see...that there is
in all the things of earth a
hidden glory waiting to be
revealed, more glorious than
a million suns.

—David Bentley Hart
The Doors of the Sea,
(Eerdmans, 2005) p. 102

Enjoying Life in a Coastal Village

We had owned a vacation house in Yachats since 1981, which property we sold when opportunity came to buy a lot right on the bluff. On that lot, 811 Ocean View Drive, we built a new house in 1984, and made it our primary residence in1988, selling our Newberg Spaulding Oaks apartment and the last portions of "Bryce Acres" in the Springbrook area. So, by the year 1993 we had become acclimated to coastal living, enjoying the beach with its tide pools and sandy coves, occasional storms, and migrating whales, in a generally mild, if sometimes rainy, climate. One winter, though, 1996, the temperature dropped to six degrees, snow covered the eerily silent highway, and some of our plants froze.

Fern enjoyed her quilting group at the Presbyterian Church and felt rewarded for her efforts by the gratitude of recipients—parents taking newborn babies home from the Newport birthing center. Breakfasts at the Blue Whale Café

provided affinity with neighbors who gathered periodically. We welcomed family and friends who often stayed with us. Fern and I enjoyed certain annual events in Yachats: the smelt fry; and the annual concert when a busload of senior devotees of the arts came from San Francisco to enjoy, with us local folks, classical music rendered by professional singers either on their way up the ladder of success or on the way down—the want-to-bes" and the "has-beens." The Fourth of July was celebrated with evening fireworks and a "lah de dah" parade that featured council members riding a manure spreader pulled through town by Larry Nixon's old John Deere tractor. What this parade lacked in length it made up for in uniqueness! The community celebrated each Advent season with a service at the historic "Little Log Church" museum. On this occasion the mayor would read a proclamation formally opening the season. Under "culturally correct" pressures, the event got relabeled a "winter festival" instead of a Christmas festival, but as mayor I continued to read an Advent poem along with my formal proclamation.

The local Presbyterian church included a number of affiliate members and attendees whose accustomed and primary church affinity, like ours, lay elsewhere. I recall how once the dignified Presbyterian worship was broken by a loud "Amen." It seems a Pentecostal brother resonated passionately with the pastoral message. We liked that! I preached there on occasion. Once, in November, I reminded the congregation of the biblical exhortation to "pray for those in authority" which we then did, going down a list that included not only our national leaders, but state, county, and city ones as well. After I had prayed for council members I asked if someone in the congregation would offer prayer for the mayor. One local resident responded, standing up and offering a moving and helpful prayer for me.

Following a pattern possibly initiated by St. Francis, each summer, partnering with the local pastor, we offered a "Blessing of the Animals" event outdoors on the Commons. These were delightful and spiritually moving occasions. People, some of whom never darkened a church door, brought their beloved pets, mostly dogs and cats, but occasionally a horse, a ferret or a bird. Cats, crouching in cages, hated every minute! Forgive them, Lord! In contrast, dogs frisked happily about, tugging on leashes, socializing, barking, tails a-wagging, and generally relishing the event. One cat, however, a huge, thirty-pound Maine short tail, un-caged, strutted about, intimidating the dogs! For the ceremony I read appropriate Scripture affirming God's creation and human stewardship, a local veterinarian talked about animal health issues, and then the pastor and I circled about to paired pets and owners to offer a blessing and a prayer.

We enjoyed taking scenic tours along the coast. We frequently drove up the winding road to Cape Perpetua, just a few miles south of town. On his voyage north on March 7, 1778, Captain Cook sighted this picturesque high point of the Oregon Coast on the calendar day that commemorates the martyrdom of an early Christian; so he dubbed the rocky tor St. Perpetua. Perpetua was a twenty-two-year-old nursing mother married to a nobleman when she was arrested for her Christian faith during the severe persecution under Emperor Severus, probably in AD 203. She was imprisoned briefly along with her personal servant, Felicitas, who was pregnant and gave birth in prison shortly before the two women, with others, were hauled to the arena. There, before a crowd of cheering spectators, these two steadfastly Christian women were chased and mauled by wild animals, and then executed by sword. As you might guess, this church historian made sure the story behind the name was available in the visitor center, inasmuch as somewhere along the line the saintly appellation got trashed.

During these bonus Yachats years Fern and I continued playing golf together. We gleaned agates, jasper, petrified wood, and other semi-precious stones from the beach during low tide and I polished them in a tumbler. It took about three weeks, using a series of coarse and fine grits. Some were pebble sized, others as large as four inches across. We gave away many (sometimes as useful worry stones to rub); others remain in our possession, as decorative items.

I also continued my hobby of restoring wood furniture. An example that sits in our living room is a sturdy, old, solid-wood, oak occasional chair I had discovered in a neighbor's house. Mr. Dudley was dying, and when I visited him I'd sit on this battered old chair, carefully avoiding splinters. Dudley's reverse mortgage had nearly exhausted his estate, his wife had predeceased him, and there were no direct heirs. One day he just passed away peacefully. Another neighbor served as executor of the mostly diminished estate, and he gladly gave me the old chair. It took hours of work to restore it to original beauty and utility, but now it can last another century.

Enjoying Life in a Retirement Community

As noted earlier, we moved to Friendsview Retirement Community in Newberg, Oregon, December 1, 2003. Our third floor apartment faces to the northeast, catching the morning sun briefly most of the year. Our home overlooks Hess Creek canyon, with its winding trail amidst verdant trees and flowering shrubs. To the northeast we see the wooded Zimri Drive area of Springbrook where we lived for many years, and to the northwest we view Chehalem Mountain, along whose roads we have enjoyed automobile rides, often up to Bald Peak, where long ago we drove as college students less interested in scenery than in romance. (That peak is no longer bald; over the decades trees have grown back green and tall.) So we traded ocean beauty for forest beauty. Both reflect the glory of God's creation.

Living in an apartment amongst many people took some getting used to! After all the years living in a single house, we felt rather penned in. At first dining room chatter dinned in our impaired ears. With hundreds of folks living around us, many of them acquaintances, how, and to what degree, to socialize became a challenge for us—and for our neighbors, of course. The presence of former students living here made us seem older than we felt! Some of them had been college kids living in the old vet housing over which Fern and I served as dorm parents when we came to teach at George Fox College some six decades ago. But it has been good to renew friendships from the past, and to make new ones, to celebrate each other's joys (like new great-grandchildren) and bear each other's burdens (like illness and deaths) in worship and in various community gatherings.

Monthly meetings of the resident association keep us up-to-date on management policies and implementation plans, and on what resident committees are doing. Educational forums and travel treks keep us alert and open to our world of people, things, and ideas. The burden of aging is lightened by table fellowship, sometimes serious, mostly non-political, and often humorous. The food is excellent—lots of fruits and vegetables. I found folks to play golf with, and actually learned to play pool with other old guys in the recreation center. (In 2010 I won the annual tournament.)

It has been hard to witness loss of health and mental acumen in cherished friends. It was good I could visit sister Lucille in the health center for a few years before she died. To ward off depression, we sometimes ate lunch at Izzy's—in Newberg or McMinnville. Sometimes on Saturdays we lunched at MacDonald's, mostly to watch the children play!

Using Friendsview's well-equipped shop, I stepped up my hobby of crafting clocks, choosing scrap lumber or driftwood with unusual configurations, then shaping and sanding each creation and coating it with a semi-gloss finish. I've made a hundred or more, I imagine. Sold a few, contributed many to benefit auctions, gave others to family and friends. Same for walking sticks; I've made them by the dozens, and at the time of this writing I use one of my favorites when we go for walks, and always at night or on the canyon path, and increasingly within the building.

In 2010 I restored the pulpit of the original meeting-house of the Greenleaf, Idaho, Friends community, established in 1908. It was brought over for me to refinish, a task made even more welcomed because from that pulpit came gospel truths that nourished my spirit as a child and youth. The old pulpit, replaced some years after a new meetinghouse was built in the 1940s, had been relegated to the youth center where creative kids painted it black with sprinkles! Ick!

Now the restored pulpit stands in the Greenleaf museum—another symbol of continuity of mission.

In 2004 I restored a desk used by Levi Pennington when he was president of George Fox College. This huge roll-top desk was probably made before World War I. It is now fully functional in the office of current George Fox president, Robin Baker, a tangible symbol of a continuity of educational ministry under the prayerful care of a Christian community of faith.

Restorations such as these serve as tactile-visual metaphors of God's redeeming grace, taking what to a casual eye is junk and restoring it to the beauty and enduring utility envisioned and provided by its creator. I rejoice more, of course, in the restoration of battered lives than in the restoration of battered furniture. That I may have served as God's hand of restoration for some people throughout my life is both a wonder and a joy.

One day the human resource director at Friendsview, Peggy Hanson, asked if I would craft for her a "talking stick." Of Cherokee lineage, she told me about an old tribal custom among First Nation people in which a chief in council meeting would hand a ceremonial stick—sometimes festooned with fur or eagle feathers—in turn to persons wishing to speak. Others

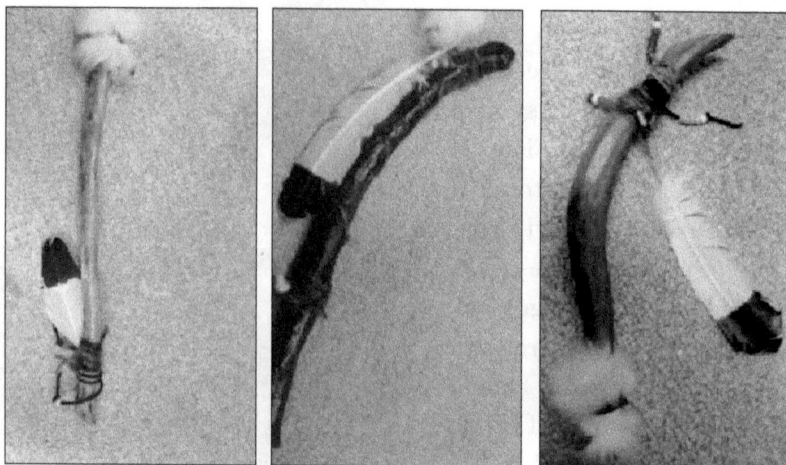

were to listen attentively, waiting their turn to hold the stick and have their verbal contribution received thoughtfully. So I crafted one for her. Friends and associates were intrigued by this aid to conciliar discussion.

I've kept the computer busy, of course. In addition to books and articles (page 140-143) occasionally I add my bit to scholarly discussions. This letter is one example:

Letter to the Editor, sent email
[not used in the next issue, although others were]

Re: Edward O. Wilson's espousal of intelligent evolution (Nov. '05 *Harvard Magazine*)

On grounds of empirical probability, rational coherence, and intuitive insight I find the hypothesis of God the creator *much more acceptable* than Wilson's hypothesis of intelligent evolution—"no goal or purpose." *That* the cosmos exists is an even more evocative teleological question than *how* it functions.

When Darwin writes about the grandeur of the evolutionary process "having been originally breathed into a few forms or into one" he refers to this planet (earth), which is a planet on the tail end of one galaxy among a hundred billion other galaxies. I find much more compelling the hypothesis of God breathing life into cosmic stuff, than the hypothesis that nothing did it originally and plans to quit the game in a few billion years.

As a philosopher I view with alarm an ethic of secular humanism, envisioning all kinds of scenarios in which unprincipled justifications for eugenic or political manipulations are employed to ensure the survival of those (deemed to be) the fittest.

So, along with billions of other folks (including John Polkinghorne, Ian Barbour, and Owen Gingerich, *et al.*) who rationally affirm the Creator and experience God existentially, I'll stick with an ancient proverb: "the fear of the Lord is the beginning of wisdom."

Arthur O. Roberts
Professor at large, George Fox University

This next letter was contributed to an online Quaker network that discusses theological subjects. It is a response to a trend among *some* liberal Friends to reject as obsolete our basic Christian foundation.

Dear Friends,

It's a puzzle to me how folks in good conscience can be members, or accept members into a Quaker meeting, claim the name and legacy of Friends, and yet reject the *foundational Christian* beliefs of George Fox, William Penn, the men and women of the "Valiant Sixty," John Woolman, Anthony Benezet, and most of the world's Friends past and present. The sometimes divisive, at other times creative, tension between liberal and conservative *Christian* Friends I can handle. But to substitute and promote outright nontheistic ideology is a grief to me.

Many years ago in a Quaker group when I waxed stridently on a poorly thought-out point, an older Friend stood up, looked at me squarely and asked: "Friend Arthur, has it ever occurred to you that you might be wrong?" I was properly chastened, silenced, and forced to acknowledge that I had been self-deceived, ego-driven into error. I thank God for this Quaker elder's pointed and compassionate query! It's a question I will put to non-theistic Quakers, and those who accept them into covenant membership (if any are reading this): "has it ever occurred to you that *you* may be wrong?" Despite the finitude of its adherents, hasn't truth "prospered" intellectually and morally more fruitfully through theism than through polytheism and atheism? Do you think Robert Barclay and Thomas Kelly meant well but were mistaken? Do you claim to understand the human psyche better than Jesus? Do you think the resurrection story is a fraud? Do you think young mother Perpetua, gored by bulls in a Roman arena, and heroic Quaker Mary Dyer, hanged on Boston Common, should have denied Christ, recanted their faith, and gone back to their families?

Have you considered that Francis Collins, of genome fame, may be right, like C. S. Lewis decades ago, in moving from atheism to agnosticism, to theism, and to experiential Christian faith? Yes, and that Jesus, some of whose teachings you admire when exemplified by Friends, might be right about the *roots* of morality as well as its fruits? And that Christians generally might be right that belief in God gives coherent meaning to life on earth—now and in the future? And that billions of galaxies testify to, and don't diminish, the wonder of God's creation?

I urge you: be content to be an earnest seeker within our faith community. Don't try to wreck it. Don't just cherish Quaker fruits while trying to chop out the roots. Presumably, you admire the Quaker testimony about integrity. Well, my friend, practice it! I urge you to acknowledge that current "idols of the tribe"—contemporary non-theistic humanism—can blot out the Light of Christ that has been drawing you into dialogue with Quakers. Please don't let this happen!

In compassionate concern, Arthur O. Robert (11/14/09)

During these bonus years I've continued to write poetry, some published, others just personal tributes, acknowledgements of lives well lived and services well rendered. Some simply reflect upon the vicissitudes of life. (See examples included in this book.)

To bolster our spirits, shortly after we moved back to Newberg, Fern spotted a sporty red Honda Accord coupe in a McMinnville dealership showroom, and in February 2004 we traded in our stodgy well-traveled sedan for this spiffier new model. We wanted what might become our last car to be a classy one. What a beauty! And it got thirty miles to the gallon! Each year we drove fewer miles. We often ventured along back roads through the beautiful countryside, sometimes out to the coast, moving over to the road shoulder if necessary to let speedsters roar past, their eyes glued to the road, alas, too busy to enjoy God's creation. Pride in things of beauty need not be sinful! The Lord has helped humble us in other ways! Better pride in good things than in grungy stuff! The good, the true and the beautiful demonstrate an excellence to which we are called of God. (The beautiful Honda did become our final car in late November 2013).

In Newberg, for several years, Fern expanded her quilting ministry. I ministered with words; she ministered with

her hands. Not only has she tied baby quilts for the local hospital, but also for the Mennonite Central Committee, a service agency we have supported financially for many years. A neighbor couple in our apartment complex is active in that service agency, so Fern channeled some quilts through them. The following note to Fern, written July 9, 2009, by MCC representative Bob Buxman, means much to us.

> Just a word of deep appreciation for the making, blessing, sending of the twelve baby comforters....Can you imagine a young mother, often poor to destitute, living in a refugee camp, receiving such a beautiful, clean, bright, new blanket upon the birth of her child created in the image of God? A very moving picture indeed. The recipients often ask "Who gives these to us?" We tell them it is people like yourselves, who have experienced God's love through Jesus Christ and want to share this love with others. Finally, and most importantly, *Jesus says thank you*, for in Matthew 25 he says, "as you have done it to the least of these...you have done it unto me," as you have wrapped a newborn in one of your comforters, you have wrapped baby Jesus himself!

One real blessing of our bonus years at Friendsview is living adjacent to the campus of George Fox University. I am no longer an austere "Dr. Roberts," but, with Fern, sort of a surrogate grandparent to some students whom we meet while walking about campus, reading in the library, sitting by them at ball games, or having lunch amongst them in the Bruin Den. Sometimes, with other donors, we enjoyed a meal with our scholarship recipients. It is interesting how some young folks welcomed our interchanges while others didn't quite know how to relate to old folks. But we smiled at all of them.

Our life has been blessed by opportunities to attend concerts in Bauman Auditorium, a short walk from our apartment. The annual Christmas musical program is indescribably beautiful—to the ear, the eye, the mind, and the soul. In

2010, 2011, and 2012 narration included selections from my book of seasonal poetry, *Look Closely at the Child*. We have enjoyed the Oregon Symphony Orchestra, community musical performances, the George Fox bands and orchestras, and student musical recitals, vocal and instrumental. At times we attended chapel and convocations. Sometimes in the summer we would walk over to watch and to hear youngsters in the Suzuki program perform their piano, cello, or violin pieces on the stage of this acoustically excellent auditorium—and to do their bows! Just a bit farther away Wood-Mar Auditorium offers an assortment of student dramatic performances.

The university baseball field is just across Hess Canyon from our Creekside residence. In the summer we can hear the bats of youth participating in Park and Recreation programs and sometimes we have walked over to watch them play. And during the spring baseball season in our early Friendsview years we went to collegiate games. We were especially grateful when some of the young men would come chat with us, accept us as surrogate grandparents, and even visit us in our apartment. And when we ate a lunch at Bruin Den, they might drop by to chat and to get a hug from Fern. We watched the team that won the NCAA Division III title in 2004. Right across the road from us is Miller Gymnasium where we enjoyed basketball games. The men do well, but in recent years the women have excelled, in 2009 winning the NCAA Division III national title without a single loss! Friendsview folks are such loyal fans; teams come over after the season to share a meal and tell their stories. We also have attended faculty lectures and assorted academic conferences.

Privileged with holding an emeritus status as "professor-at-large" I sometimes met with the Religious Studies faculty. Fern and I are invited to various academic or social functions, including Tuesday faculty lunches. Being next to the university really enriched us, as it has other members of our retirement community, many of them alumni who also enjoy the amenities of campus life. The library archives contain twenty some boxes of my professional and ministerial documents. I am grateful that the university has made this service available. Perhaps I'm being vain, but who knows, some inquisitive historically minded scholar someday may nose about in these files, hopefully not rendered obsolete by electronic storage (scholars have already utilized the *Alaska Quaker Documents*). In 2011 the administration selected me to give the undergraduate commencement address. It was an honor to be chosen. I worked hard preparing it. Entitled "Love and Truth Working Together," (see page 87) the fifteen-minute address to the graduates and their families was one of the most satisfying experiences of my public ministry, receiving plaudits and requests for copies.

Walking about the campus we observed how trees have grown since we were students here. The evergreens we planted by tennis courts and track fifty years ago are now giants—the redwoods a dozen feet or more in circumference at the base. In the forests above Newberg one sees stands of fir where thirty years go only stump land from a second harvest had been visible. One of the blessings of getting old is to watch and smell and sense growing forest life.

It was good to participate again in North Valley Friends Church, which we had helped establish decades earlier, and, as we were able, to participate in Wednesday night suppers and classes. It blessed our hearts to see young families with their small children enjoying each other in the context of Christian faith and community. Generally we attended the 9:30 a.m. Sunday meeting for worship. It is adapted from an older Quaker model: after the presider reads an opening Scripture or devotional passage, we are gathered by Christ into prayerful silence, out of which some short vocal ministry may arise. Each exhortation or interpretation of Scripture truth is considered thoughtfully. We conclude with prayers for shared concerns or needs. This small group (15-25 persons) was helpful inasmuch as apartment living and daily mingling with many folks at Friendsview, although beneficial in some ways, made us cherish a small group for worship. We appreciate the pastoral care and fellowship.

Friendsview holds Sunday morning services, which we attended after we quit driving. From time to time I am asked to bring the message at the midweek meeting. (By 2013 I had preached a couple dozen times.) Although less involved than previously in committee work and programs of Northwest Yearly Meeting of Friends Church, I did contribute some leadership, for example preaching a sermon at the annual sessions in 2006, posting "Reflections" on the pastors' website monthly for a dozen years, and occasionally mentoring younger scholars pursuing advanced degrees. My books and articles, of course, also minister to this extended church family.

A great joy of these latter years has been family visits. We count each additional year together as a bonus from the Lord. Our children and grandchildren (scattered and busy) visit as often as they can, and relish family dinners at Friendsview, sharing experiences and just being together. Seeing our great-grandchildren grow from babyhood to school years is a delight. We enjoyed a sixtieth wedding anniversary celebration in 2003, a family picnic on July 30, 2011, birthday parties in 2010, and a beautiful seventieth anniversary celebration in 2013! Phone calls and email (and even Skype) augment communication, but at birthdays and Christmas, letters are exchanged. This old writer occasionally creates a poem to celebrate a birthday or other special event. We cherish all forms of family contacts, including parting hugs and prayer together. Great-grandchildren find the Friendsview garden a fun place. They enjoy seeing the flowers, pulling up fresh carrots in season, or plucking a few blueberries. Their parents enjoy beating grandpa at pool.

2009 was the year we acknowledged that we had grown old. Heavy colds took a toll on us physically that winter and again a year later during the month of February. We quit our drives into Portland and began to avoid freeways and major highways, delighting, rather, in moseying along country roads after worship on Sundays, or on sunny days. (In January 2013 I renewed my driver's license, but as noted, quit driving that fall.) Our walks and drives became shorter each year. I haven't played golf since 2009. So far we have not used wheeled walkers—a popular form of assistance here. I've been sorting out and discarding stuff, like old philosophy syllabi and lecture notes. I won't need them and no one else will either. All part of the aging process.

In early 2011 we reduced participation in outside events, watching some ball games and chapel events by "live streaming" on the computer screen instead of going across the street. In 2011 Fern decided she had made enough baby quilts in thirty years, so she gave away sewing stuff. (But she did shorten my trousers that seemed to have gotten longer over the years!)

On January 3, 2011, I had a pacemaker implanted to correct a slow pulse. It took a bit of time for my body to adjust, but it certainly helped mobility. But in that year we both felt the aging process, so we went less often to North Valley for worship and fellowship, or across to George Fox for events. In early February 2012 I suffered a gall bladder attack, was hospitalized a few days, medicated heavily to curb infection, subjected to various medical procedures including a stress test, followed by laparoscopic surgery on February 29. It took care of the problem. It seems February is our aging month! We have had to cope with decreasing strength and energy. No major health problems at the time of this writing, however, just diminishing energy.

Although the years ahead loom short the days seem long. Fern handles reduced activity better than I. The Lord, thankfully, has led me through this dark valley.

Puttering Around

Lord, I don't have much to do these days.
Meals are provided, apartment cleaned.
Don't feel up to working in the shop.
The weather's too stormy for a drive.
My eyes get blurry and my head
achy after an hour of reading
˙ (maybe I need new glasses).
I've finished two crossword puzzles.
My writing project is completed.
Since my surgery I've not felt up
to playing much pool, either.
Can't nap in the day,
Too tense, I guess.
Lord, I'm an old man coping
with long days and restless nights.
Fearful that my life may be
closing down here on earth,
and loath to let it go. So,
with the Psalmist I pray
"Lord, deliver me from my fears."
And he does. Reminds me, through
my dear wife and loving family
that we have much
to be thankful for. We do.
So help me to live for today,
nor anxious be....

41

We enjoy our apartment with its view of the canyon and hills. Fern is right: "We have much to be thankful for!" We play lots of Scrabble, read books and magazines and enjoy our evening drink of Ensure. We thank the Lord our minds are reasonably intact (albeit a bit pokey, remiss at remembering names), although our bodies are perceptibly aging. We have each other. Our love is strong. Our faith, though challenged, remains healthy. Praise the Lord!

Reflections

A couple of furniture drawers are filled with memorabilia. Over the years we just shoved things into this collection. From time to time we look at them. Why did we keep all this stuff anyway? One weathered article is Fern's autograph booklet from Louisiana times.

Many entries are the usual middle school silliness, but this one, dated October 18, 1934, deserves the light of day: "When many a year has long rolled by; and upon this page you cast your eye; remember it was a friend sincere, who left her sweet remembrance here."

There's worse ways to get old than rummaging around in your memories.

Jon Hassler, *North of Hope* (Ballantyne, 1990) p. 347)

(Simple verse but better than some of the stuff I read in the *New Yorker*.) It's signed by Ethel Marchand, of 511 Wiltz Street, Rayne. (This town is called the "Frog Capitol of the World"; Fern remembers eating frog legs there!) In one drawer is a red sports letter "G" standing for Greenleaf academy. It was the custom in olden days to sew this emblem onto sweaters to show status as a ball player, along with arm stripes for the number of years on the team. I can't recall what happened to my old college letterman's sweater—some things just disappear, although images linger in the mind. Oh, here is a brochure narrating the 1951 Kansas City flood. From the office building where she worked, Fern escaped the rapidly rising waters in a boat. Exciting!

This packet of love letters is interesting! I expect our kids and grandkids might get a kick out of them, if they don't shred them first. In one dated June 30, 1942, Fern writes to me at the logging camp near Colton, Oregon, where Wayne Roberts and I labored that hot summer. Fern tells about her work in the Springbrook cannery, then pretends jealousy about Florence (the matronly camp cook and cigarette roller) and closes with "As ever—only more so!" Ah, love was blooming between us! Some later letters—and entries in Fern's diary—are mushier so we'll not narrate these syrupy sentiments. Suffice it to say we were engaged that Christmas and married the next fall. Nice memories to rummage around in!

Passing On a Legacy

From time to time we mailed our grandchildren pastoral reflections. Whether they seemed too "preachy" or not, we'll never know. The kids were pretty quiet about them—hopefully from pondering the words thoughtfully—occasionally expressing appreciation. But these reflections did two things anyway; they put in tangible form aspects of our spiritual legacy, and they demonstrated love—we cared enough to convey this legacy to them. Here are a few of them.

"What did we learn from our grandparents?"

From your grandfather:
Today, the story is about our grandparents. I didn't know my mother's parents. Mother Jansonius, a widow, lived in Iowa. I vaguely remember meeting her. My father's mother, Mary Bevan, widow of Levi Roberts, lived about twenty-five miles away, at Star, Idaho, in a little "grandma" house next to her banker son's spacious home. I saw her occasionally. She died when I was a young child. What did I learn from her? Well, the value of an inheritance. Her father had invested wisely in property, and these family funds enabled my uncle Ervin to set up a small bank and my father, Owen, to purchase farm property, first in the Riverside area in Southern Idaho and then in the Pleasant Ridge community, closer to the Greenleaf Quaker community and its meetinghouse and academy.

More importantly, grandmother Mary transmitted the family Quaker heritage, one that goes back to the mid-1600s, with our Welsh ancestors finding religious freedom in Penn's colony in the 1690s. I am very grateful for this.

She was a strong Christian and a recognized Friends leader. She was also a poet. Somewhere I have one of her poems. My mother sometimes chafed a bit at how matriarch Mary catered to my father—her little boy! But I guess mothers (and fathers) continue to just be like that, even as their children mature and themselves become parents and grandparents.

From your grandmother:

I don't have many memories of my father's mother, Emma Nixon Byerley. She divorced my father's father, John Nixon, when my dad was a boy. My dad lived most of his early life in Scappoose, Oregon, with his father. As a child I saw this grandmother only once (we were living in Long Beach, California). In 1930 my folks moved to the Springbrook, Oregon, area. Byerleys lived there two years and then returned to Rickreal. Grandma Beyerly died shortly thereafter.

My mother's mother—Dulcie Mae (Harrington) Faith—lived near Lawndale, California. Surnames from previous marriages were Maxson and Schermer. She made many dresses for Viola and me—cutting her own pattern! We would see a dress we liked and Grandma would make one for us—a wonderful seamstress. She would take us on the electric streetcar into Los Angeles to the May company and let us ride up and down the escalator (a novelty for us). We always went there for the Christmas gala. She made wonderful milk toast. When we were sick we always wanted to go to grandma's house. She had a wonderful feather bed and a special "sick blanket." When I visited her in 1948 I discovered she had kept my mud pies (in a rabbit hutch)! When she was about eighty-five and unable to care for herself, she came to Oregon and lived in a care home in the Dallas area. Hers was the gift of loving Christian service!

"What did we learn from our parents?"

From your grandfather:

My father, Owen Roberts, in the early 1900s, had moved with his mother and brother's family from Iowa to newly irrigated

Boise valley, Idaho, a desert beginning to blossom with acres of alfalfa, barley, and herds of cattle. Owen was a forty-year-old bachelor, so sister Mae matched him up with a thirty-year-old teacher, Bertha Jansonius, who had left settled Iowa for adventures out West. Well, the romance worked. I was the fourth living child of this marriage (following Lucille, Marjorie, and Warren), born when my father was fifty and my mother forty. From my father I learned to respect God's earth and its creatures. He was gentle with horses and cattle. And with us! The only spanking I ever got was after I robbed a robin's nest and mashed her eggs down a neighbor girl's neck (my abuse of the mother bird really ticked him off). Papa even hummed hymns like "Amazing Grace" while slopping hogs! (At thirteen I thought it weird!) From papa I learned the value of spiritual disciplines like daily Bible reading and table prayers. I learned staunch Quaker values such as honest dealings, conscientious labor, owning fewer but better things, and avoiding debt.

My mother, from a Presbyterian family, was more vocal in her faith. She taught us kids spiritual habits: bedtime prayers, the Lord's Prayer at Sunday dinner, the Westminster Catechism, and the ABCs of the Bible (A. "All have sinned and come short of the glory of God"; B. "Behold the Lamb of God who takes away the sin of the world," etc.). A wall painting of Jesus holding little children helped us visualize what we sang in Sunday school: "Jesus loves the little children of the world, red and yellow, black and white, all are precious in his sight." Mom's family members were enterprising Dutch immigrants. Education was important. So we kids read books, used the local Carnegie library, practiced penmanship, took music lessons, and earned college degrees. Before we could drive, she hauled us in the green Model A Ford to Sunday evening youth meetings. (We kids thought she drove too fast! Over forty, probably.)

From your grandmother:

My mother, Mae Maxson Nixon, demonstrated a remarkable capacity to adapt to circumstances. I grew up in Long Beach, California, where Mom had a beauty shop. When dad moved the family from California to the Louisiana oil fields, she adapted to muggy, humid weather for a time but eventually got my father to move back west. My parents bought a small farm near Newberg (where the A-Dec dental equipment manufacturing plant is now located). To help meet expenses mom did seasonal work at the Springbrook cannery. She got us to attend the Springbrook Friends church and participate in its youth activities. Arthur and I were married in that church. Its building was taken down when the congregation merged with another to become North Valley Friends. We salvaged the "deacon's bench" which Trish keeps in her home.

My father, Guy Nixon, was a soft-hearted man, gentle with us children (and later with grandchildren). He met and married mother upon his return to Dallas, Oregon, from service in World War I. He had driven a munitions truck in France. Pa never said much about the war, other than this: "If old men had to fight they would find another way to settle things!" During my growing-up years he was a heavy drinker—sometimes scaring us kids. Military stress? Job frustration? Who knows? But in Newberg he patiently worked his land, milked the cows, did seasonal cannery work, and encouraged us as we walked the tracks to college. After Viola and I both married, the folks sold this farm and purchased a dairy near Battle Ground, Washington. After a few years they retired to a small filbert farm near Newberg. In his latter years dad finally committed his life to Jesus Christ, and with God's help quit drinking.

Handling Doubt

During growing up years you may have experienced religious doubt. Maybe a teacher scoffed at Christian faith, or questioned its compatibility with science, or you were irked by religious leaders whose lurid sins got hyped in the press. Or, you heard others tell about spiritual experiences you hadn't had. Or, you wanted to hide guilty feelings. But you didn't tell grandpa about these doubts because you love him and didn't want to hurt his feelings. Or you felt intimidated by his professorial status, and/or you wanted to avoid a lecture. In any case, here are some things I have learned—and experienced— about doubt. *Because you do love me,* please consider them thoughtfully. We can talk about them if you wish.

There are two sorts of doubts. The first kind of doubt is just the underside of faith, wondering how what we believe makes sense—faith seeking to understand. We love God with our minds, as well as our hearts, but often minds crave reassurance—especially when challenged by disbelief. Jesus' disciples doubted his resurrection until he appeared among them. Jesus told Thomas, "blessed are those who have not seen but believe." (That includes us.) Faith doesn't mean being irrational. Not at all! Faith provides a *context for reason*. Belief in God is sustained rationally by the Bible's witness, by historic Christian teachings, and by personal testimony. Faith in God offers logical, coherent meaning *both to nature and to human life*. This first sort of doubt actually strengthens faith by clarifying truth.

The second sort of doubt is different. It's a subtle form of self-deception. It involves using one's mind to rationalize evil conduct rather than conscientiously to seek and follow truth. It's easier to lie or cheat if we convince ourselves God doesn't exist, or doesn't bother about us, or that the story of Jesus means little to us "enlightened" folks. And so, moral doubters welcome pop literature that debunks the gospel, or turn to religious groups that massage the ego but don't call for ethical accountability or Christian discipleship.

Some folks experience *both* sorts of doubt at the same time! And in their depressing darkness they need loving persons to come beside them and help them regain a steady faith in God and in themselves. Sometimes ecstatic experiences of God's presence just override doubt and confirm faith. We can't schedule such spiritual highs; but from time to time God just overwhelms us with his presence and we are filled with joy for sins forgiven and/or for the sheer beauty of walking the path of life with Jesus. Cherish such occasions! But know that in the long haul we are sustained by a quiet, steady faith in God.

Grammy concurs with this reflection and sends her love, too.

August 15, 2012

Dear grandchildren,

I expect you watched some Olympic events—maybe cheering for the US volleyball team, enjoying gymnastics, or seeing Murray defeat Federer at tennis. (How the Brits cheered!) The symbol of the Olympic games is composed of five interlocking rings—blue, yellow, black, green, and red—on a white field. Wikipedia informs us that the symbol was designed in 1912 by Baron Pierre de Coubertin, founder of the modern Olympics. Twenty-eight nations participated. The idealism that prompted this—sport as alternative to war—got blunted by World War I, but persisted in the hearts of people throughout the world.

Using the Olympics symbol as a model for affinity circles, we can say that Gabriel and Rigel are now in the middle of a center circle—family—like you were when we grandparents cuddled you! Our other great-grandchildren are already reaching out and gradually, like parents before them, will move toward the periphery of the family circle, and eventually form new affinities—interlocking circles.

What are the other circles? Let's call the gold one *guiding beliefs*, the green one *vocation* (school, work, shared community tasks), the blue one *friendship*, the red one *nation*.

Please ponder these circles. Ask yourself questions. How can I honor the family groups that nurtured me? How can I sustain the Christian beliefs that shaped and nurtured them? How can I maintain integrity on my job? How can I make and retain mutually supportive friendships? How can I help my country achieve its democratic goals of justice for all?

Thank you, dear grandchildren, for loving us—and for accepting counsel. Please keep in touch by email, phone, or letter, and, when possible, by personal visits. We love you!

Grandpa Roberts

With Mystical Power

Light, softened by a tinge of red,
streams through the bedroom window.
The old man shakes off dreams,
and wakens. He puts his shaky hand
gently on her shoulder. She rouses,
adjusts covers, and slips into his arms,
snuggling close to her beloved.
Wrapped all warm and cozy,
together they greet the new day,
breathing thanks to the Lord for it.
They lie there caressing each other
as the sun rises over the horizon.
Sometimes they nod off for a while.
Few words are spoken—or needed.
With mystical power, touch articulates
the joys from seventy years of love.

Fill, brief or long, my granted span
of life with love of thee and man;
strike when thou wilt the hour of rest.
But let my last days be my best.

—John Greenleaf Whittier, "The Clear Vision"
(Poetry, Jolliff edition, Friends United Press, 2000)

Yes, Lord!

DECADE ONE. Do not fear the dark, my boy. Say 'amen' and
hop into bed! I am with you during the night as well
as during the day. Go to sleep, my precious child. *Yes, Lord!*

DECADE TWO. You may fool your parents, my son, but not me. What
you did is sin. Repent; receive my forgiveness. I have called you
to minister. Will you follow me, now? *Yes, Lord!*

DECADE THREE. My son, preaching is more than rhetoric;
ministry means speaking gospel truth first to self, then to
gathered worshipers and visitors. Will you do so? *Yes, Lord!*

DECADE FOUR. My son, beware subtle self-deception. Wisdom
is more than knowledge. I called you to serve family,
students, and associates, not to inflate ego. Right? *Yes, Lord!*

DECADE FIVE. In troubled times truth overcomes deceit; love
overcomes hate. So, my son, will you convey this message
with cogent words and compassionate deeds? *Yes, Lord!*

DECADE SIX. My son, some student faces convey concerns beyond
course mastery. Will you discern ways to tender such
troubled youth appropriate counsel and comfort? *Yes, Lord!*

DECADE SEVEN. My son, I have called you to write and speak
for the sake of truth, not for public applause. Will you
be diligent, disciplined, and devoted to your calling? *Yes, Lord!*

DECADE EIGHT. My son, retirement doesn't free you from
social responsibility. Will you serve by helping govern this
pleasant town, so peace and justice will prevail? *Yes, Lord!*

DECADE NINE. My son, grandchildren are a blessing. As patriarch
will you wrap your pearls of wisdom in love, and pray each day
for these young adults and their families? *Yes, Lord!*

DECADE TEN. Do not fear lengthening shadows, my dear friend. Enjoy extended family and friendship circles. I'll meet
you at your new home some bright morning. *Yes, Lord! Yes!*

(previously published in Daring to Grow,
Northwest Yearly Meeting Board of Christian Education, 2013)

Recent
Poetry and Prose

I'll share a few poems written during bonus years. Because of its timeliness, January 2009, the first one got circulated widely on the Internet, eliciting many commendations. The poems reflect various moods—silly, sad, reflective, evocative, satirical, commemorative, and exultant.

Prayer for President Obama

Lord God, we pray for President Barack Obama.
We praise you for the gifts you have nurtured in him:
to think clearly, to speak eloquently, to interact effectively.
Guide him, God, to use these skills both wisely and well
as he leads our nation and serves our world.

Thank you for his bright summons to audacious hope.
May we citizens bracket that vision with faith and love,
so that civility and justice mark our nation's journey
into an unknown and somewhat scary future.

May the glare of publicity never blind him to truth.
May political power never dull empathy with ordinary people.
May pride of position never corrode his conscience.
Warn him, Lord, when evils, disguised as good,
tempt him to stray from what is right and true.

Teach him to backtrack from wrong turns amiably,
but to follow right roads tenaciously.
Strengthen his commitment to servant leadership.
May neither acclaim nor criticism tarnish his congeniality.

Show him patterns of patience that tarry but do not dawdle.
When he is tired and stressed, refresh him, Lord,
in his body, in his mind, in his spirit.
When alone he wrestles over difficult ethical and policy issues
may this follower of Jesus heed his Master's guiding voice.

Oh, and Lord, in busy times remind President Obama
of his heart-felt pledge and studied practice:
to be an attentive and loving husband and father.

Benedictory Prayer

Dear God, on this inaugural occasion
we pray for President Baker. Bless him!
Grant this historian wisdom to apply
time-tested insights and traditions
within the current, conflicted culture.
Stand with him on introspective peaks
and point out *your* paths for education
within, and through, a murky future.
Help him to articulate this vision, Lord,
to all of us at George Fox University.
Working at an historic roll-top desk,
and living in a pioneer Quaker home
signify a valued continuity of vision.
May he give substance to these symbols,
Lord, conjoining spirit, mind, and body.
Guard him against self-deceptions
that subtly blind the eye to truth.

Oh God, may neither pride of place
nor perquisites of power ever impair
this loving servant leader, Robin.
Help him to discern what actions,
are central to our school's service,
and, Lord, how to implement them
effectively, with biblical stewardship
of resources, human and material.
We pray for President Baker's family.
For Ruth, wife, hostess, mother.
And, Lord, we pray for their children,
for Jacob, for Rebekah, for Tara.
Lead them down your paths, too.
In Jesus' name, Amen.

"Right for You"

Ponder with me, good folks out there,
a frequently-urged commercial admonition:
"Ask your doctor if it's right for you!"
Right for you! Not someone else, right for you!
A reassuring fatherly voice reminds us that
this medicine "is not for everyone," including
lesser souls who suffer one or more ailments
delineated rapidly in such sweetly dulcet tones
you know it's right for you, especially as a smiling—
if slightly smirking—couple embrace to show
the happiness this medical wonder brings.
It's such a faithful affirmation of our trust
in the guiding principle of individualism,
that our bodies ache for this healing balm,
and our minds eagerly respond:
"we'll call the doctor in the morning."

A Cheerful Red

[2004 Honda Accord coupe]

Celebrating sixty years of marriage
merits more than cake and punch
on a Saturday afternoon.
Let's buy a new car! A spiffy one,
not one of those boxy things
the grandkids consider so cool.
Again we crave beautiful wheels.
So we purchased a new Honda coupe,
a classy car with leather upholstery,
a cheerful red, like the Mercury
we bought nearly fifty years before.
Well, we won't drive it as fast
or as far as we did that big Merc.
Red's a great color for people
who need, and ought, to be seen
as young in heart when they're
no longer young in years!
This car, too, should serve a decade
until our next major anniversary.
"Swing low, sweet chariot!"

O, Yes, It's Ray

Why do I forget names?
Well, my brain has gotten
sort of pokey lately,
just like my legs.
It takes a bit of effort
to pull my body upright.
The same with my brain.
If I relax a bit and don't fuss,
a psycho-physiological flunky
will hoist himself from his couch,
amble down neural aisles of memory
and, hopefully, locate the right document,
in the right file. It's there, somewhere,
stored amid stacks and stacks of data,
some of it junk, better forgotten,
but refusing to stay trashed.
And, if I am patient, my helpful techie
will bring out a picture album
about this nearly forgotten friend.
These sensory memories
help me to recall names.
Oh, yes, it's Ray!

The Eighth D-mension

1. Lord, deliver me from the depths of disobedience.
   I've been deceitful, defiant, devilish.
   And now, I am down in the dumps.
   > My child, I forgive you. Go and sin no more!
   > Accept divine deliverance.

2. Lord, deliver me from the depths of discord.
   Our group is ravaged by division, and disruption.
   I'm deserted by persons I depended on.
   > My child, lift up your head, be at peace!
   > Accept divine deliverance.

3. Lord, deliver me from the depths of depression.
   I am despondent; I wallow in dejection.
   I feel numb inside, and dumb outside.
   > My child, feast your eyes upon my world!
   > Accept divine deliverance.

4. Lord, deliver me from the depths of despair.
   I am desperate, desolate, lonely, direction-less.
   Discouragement dogs me daily.
   > My child, here I am: take my hand!
   > Accept divine deliverance.

5. Lord, deliver me from the depths of dishonor,
   deficient in duty, dubbed a "dumb" cluck,
   I've been deposed, discredited, depersonalized.
   > My child, let love and truth empower you!
   > Accept divine deliverance.

6. Lord, deliver me from the depths of disbelief.
I am double-minded, praying while doubting,
discounting doctrines but disdaining cynics.
> My child, faith has eyes to see truth whole!
> Accept divine deliverance.
7. Lord, deliver me from the depths of disability.
I am diminished in body, dependent on others,
afraid of becoming demented.
> My child, rest soul and body in my care!
> Accept divine deliverance.
8. Lord, I delight in your presence.
You dipped down deep in my soul to deliver.
I depend now on your Spirit to define my way.
> In devotion my heart sings each day.
> O my Lord! Joy, demonstrable joy.

God's Lifting Power

I wonder on what star-filled night
an oak tree's sturdy trunk and roots
cracked and broke a concrete slab
of campus sidewalk where I walk.
I marvel at how patiently
the tree presses, lifting, lifting,
until, fearing folks might trip
upon the rising edge, someone
removes the jagged slab to lay
a new one several feet away.
I wonder on what star-filled night
kingdom strength will crack and break
my carelessly constructed path
through life. Before I trip and fall—
or others do—I ask God's angel
to remove that broken piece
and lay a new path for my feet,
conformable to truth and love.
Penitently at this Advent hour
I would discern God's lifting power.

That Old Fir Tree

At canyon's edge an old fir tree
highlights our east landscape view.
Last year a woodsman climbed high up
and sawed off a rotting top.
Below this cut a new lead branch
stretches its spring candles skyward—
one year, two years, three years, four—
more? Unlikely! Scraggly branches
bare of needles mark the side
where sustenance was sacrificed
to pave a needed parking space,
but others, too, are turning gray.
Self-giving service marks the beauty
of this old fir now. Woodpeckers
feast on bugs dug from the bark.
Birds seek shelter in the holes,
squirrels frolic round and round
the weathered trunk. Lacking foliage,
it won't topple in those gales
that sometimes maim younger ones.
How we cherish that fir tree!

To the Green Hills

As the day dawned dank and grey,
my mood matched the soggy weather:
not warm and sunny but damp and chilly,
uninviting to self as well as to others.
The blustering clouds overhead
seemed to hover darkly within me.
I shivered, and persons around me
wrapped sweaters more closely
about them. Oh, no! I sighed,
is this how to be glad "in the day
that the Lord hath made"?
I lifted my eyes up to the green hills,
(like my loved ones, flourishing).
"Forgive me, Lord," I cried. Then sunlight
flooded my soul on this rainy day.

Tribute to Mackey Hill

I give tribute today to Mackey Hill,
long-time collegiate colleague,
historian, custodian of centuries
of human thought and conduct,
the good, the bad, and that puzzling
mixture of both. As a cartographer
of the human trek in space and time,
this earnest, studious, follower of Jesus
helped generations of students
to understand the human pilgrimage,
to gain a heavenly perspective,
to find good paths for their own feet.
If we mark time by centuries
his hundred years among us
are indeed memorable.
Thank you Mackey Hill.

Tribute to Fred and Mardella Newkirk

Thank you, Fred and Mardella,
for forty years of compassionate ministry.
You focus God's light upon lives
blighted by urban darkness.
You open a door of hope for folks
who've had doors slammed in their faces.
Beguiled by serpentine voices within and without,
they've been entrapped by sin and trashed
by a society preoccupied with material success.
In sorrow, yes, and in anger, you witness
the drug-death march along inner city streets;
then you gather them in—meth-ed up mothers,
derelict dads, defiant sons, delinquent daughters,
battered children, crime victims and victimizers.
In your basement Bible study for the broken
you map the road to heaven for them,
you introduce them to their true guide, Jesus.
Thank you, Fred and Mardella!
We're all sinners, rich and poor alike,
down but by God's grace not out,
not wasted, but forgiven and redeemed!
Praise God! Praise God for victory
over sin and despair and death,
through our Lord Jesus Christ!

"Truth has Prospered"

I give tribute to Dean Freiday, devoted theologian,
who taught us, locally and around the world,
that the church is *Nothing Without Christ.*
Within a culture of unbelief, he has proclaimed
biblically, rationally, and experientially,
"Christ is still the answer."
Sandy's "Jim" was a meticulous scholar.
As one friend observed, Dean could
"stuff Quaker theology into a 1000 word package."
But also, by patient research and good writing,
he clarified for many folks normative Quaker faith
by publishing in modern English the writings of
the renowned seventeenth-century scholar, Robert Barclay,
by papers and dialogue at various conferences,
and by editing *Quaker Religious Thought.*
How reassuring for all of us, that, indeed,
Christ, the incarnate Word of God,
the "universal and saving Light,"
is still the answer! What a boon to us
earnest but sometimes confused Quakers!
In ecumenical circles Dean Freiday shared
seminal Quaker insights and strengthened
bonds with Catholic, Orthodox, and Protestant
Christians. Surely, under Dean's ministry,
from Manasquan to Bujumbura,
"Truth has prospered!"

"I Like Being Ten!" [to Zain]

Once I was a baby, then a tiny tyke,
age one, then two, three, four, five,
just having fun, glad to be alive.
At six I began to use my mind, like
on games and grade school stuff,
using numbers to figure things out,
and words for what I think about.
Seven and eight and nine were tough.
But I learned more how things work,
and why at times they don't, and when.
Now that I'm a Scout, and at age ten,
I love to learn. Who wants to be a jerk?
I yearn to learn more about our world,
how to use it right and how to share
it with other folks. Thanks, Lord, I care
about your wonderful created world!

Cheers

Cheers for a young lad named Aiden,
who likes Florida's surf to wade in,
and, to great-grandpa's delight,
he's learning to read and to write.
Keep it up, soccer player Aiden!

To Trask

Happy birthday, little baby,
born to Heidi and Sean
April 11, 2009. How wonderful
that you were born just a day
before Easter! May God
who raised Jesus from the grave
draw you into that good life
our Lord graciously offers,
during your years on earth,
and then, with us, in heaven.

To Laura and James

The substance of romance
can't be measured easily,
like teaspoons to the cup,
or counting tree rings.
These never tally up
what a good life brings
when love grows faithfully
through time and circumstance.

Life now and life tomorrow
is measured by the beauty
that love, sun-like, bestows
wherever human needs
arise. Such love shows
itself in thoughtful deeds
and through civic duty—
it triumphs over sorrow.

May this romantic love
bless our common life
like sweetly fragrant flowers
that cense a smoggy day
like welcomed summer showers
that cleanse a dusty way.
Softly, love quells strife,
When blessed by God above.

[at their wedding, 2009]

To April and Eric

It's a mystery how human love works.
A man and a woman find each other
amid ordinary life activities,
partly by chance, partly by choice.
First they venture simple things together,
dining out, movies, attending church,
taking walks, chatting about jobs,
discussing current events.
Trust develops. The two share their hopes,
fears, disappointments, aspirations.
Increasingly bodies feel good together.
Having traversed different paths,
minds get in synch, too. In all this they are
quietly nudged along by the Holy Spirit
to keep blending each with the other,
heightening respect. They share adventures,
dreams, faith in God, social concerns.
Hand in hand with each other and with God
they stand before commitment's holy altar,
in a community of friends and family,
to pledge their troth in solemn vows.
In the beautiful mystery of love
Eric and April truly have become one:
husband and wife. Together.

[at their wedding, 2010]

Far and Near

We've viewed Norway's fiords, New Zealand's
Milford Sound, the "land of fire and ice,"
the incredible terra cotta soldiers of Xian,
Alaska's arctic winter beauty,
the Grand Canyon, Niagara Falls,
Crater Lake, the Austrian Alps.
These scenic spots and many more
loom far away in time and space,
but cherished in memory and picture.
Scenes we *now* view with wonder
are nearby, not miles and miles away.
Earth's beauty surrounds us daily:
sun-blessed dandelions, gladiolas,
the symmetry of maple leaves,
red berries sparkling in shrubbery
along Hess Creek walking trail,
a quilt of roses in the garden,
poplar leaves sparkling in the wind,
a squirrel busily crunching nuts,
bushy tail waving "hello" to us,
a bluebird perched atop a tree,
a farmer's field of crimson clover.
All this, plus a morning sunrise,
herald of a cosmic transfiguration,
coming some day, with beauty
beyond our mortal minds to grasp,
but, oh, so near to eyes of faith!

Glorious Joy

Happiness wants easy paths on which to walk.
But joy strides on roadways smooth or rough.
When life's path gets hard, joy just hangs tough
and clambers on and on. Joy doesn't balk
at howling winds, hot sun, or pelting rain.
Health, friends, family, tasks: these things
bless life's journey. Incredibly, joy sings
when hard trekking brings much pain.
Exult in the wonder and beauty of God's world.
Taste joy along life's path, whatever the terrain.
Celebrate this day with flags unfurled!
Sing for beauty of the earth, so heaven driven,
awaiting Christ's cosmic re-creation,
for us sinners gloriously forgiven!
Amen

Advent

"He has lifted up the humble
and scattered the proud!"
So sang Spirit-anointed Mary
to her confidant, Elizabeth,
as together these ordinary
women celebrated, in advance,
the dawning of a new age
for all humanity.
Mary couldn't envision details
about kingdom beginnings,
including her own anguish
underneath a cruel cross,
nor similar cruciform costs
for generations yet to come.
Nor could she foresee wonder
and joy at an empty tomb!

Mary could not forecast how
arrogant imperial Rome
would be brought down;
how humble, hungering, folks
in Europe, Asia, America, Africa,
and islands of the seven seas
would be lifted from ignorance,
forgiven, filled with good things.

But Mary knew the Babe
nestled in her womb was how
Israel's messianic hopes
were to be fulfilled, how God,
the Mighty One, in mercy,
was bringing salvation
to a weary, waiting world.
In joy we know this, too!

Panic Attack

Why is my head so hot?
Maybe I have a fever—better check.
No, 97.8; well I'll breathe deeply,
get out of bed and exercise a bit.
Let's see, did I take my medicine?
Maybe I got a bad batch,
like two years ago.
Where are my anxiety pills?
It's 2 a.m. Not a good time to go to
the hospital, especially on weekends.
I did this last year and they took
a bunch of tests, sedated me a bit,
and sent me home the next day.
Maybe I should call the night nurse.
Should I waken my wife?
She'll just tell me to relax.
Been through this before.
Says I have too much imagination.
Get a new writing project.
Maybe I'm a somatizer.
I'll look that up on Google.
I'll eat a saltine cracker, walk a bit
and go back to bed.
Oh, it's six o'clock—guess I dozed off.
I feel better. I bet it's the cracker....

A Birthday

A birthday is a fun-filled day,
with hugging moments
and laughing minutes
with friends who drop by.
A birthday means happy hours
with children and grandchildren,
but it also celebrates years
of accumulated wisdom,
decades of enriching experiences,
all pointing the way
(Thanks be to Christ!)
toward an eternity of joy!
Happy birthday, Cheryl!

Golden Years

Fifty years are now over and past.
Earl and Annie's years together
daily continue to swirl about us
like breezes cooling to the face,
like music resonant to the ear.
Their marriage blesses our lives
like the aroma of mint and rose,
like the savor of delicious food.
Love makes good things last.
For a man and a woman
who love each other and God,
now more than ever before,
each sunrise nourishes hope,
each sunset, flaming with joy,
offers a blessed benediction
to carry them through the night.
Family, friends, and beneficiaries
of their giftedness bask gratefully
in the radiant afterglow
of their golden years.

Birthday

Happy ninetieth birthday, Fern!
I love you more now than
sixty-nine years ago, when
we had our first date,
more than sixty-eight years ago
when at a college skating party
you wore the engagement ring.
More than sixty-seven years ago
when we were married at Springbrook
Friends Church and honeymooned
at Newport's Dorchester House.
I love you more now than
during busy, joy-filled decades
of family and professional life.
I love you in these retirement years
blessed by children, grandchildren,
great-grandchildren, friends.
I know you love me, too!

ABCs of Theology

Atonement. Through the life, death, and resurrection of Jesus we experience God's forgiveness of sins. We gain salvation through God's power, not by our own strength. Christians picture the mystery of atonement in several ways: as hostages rescued, like one satisfying a debt another cannot pay, a friend taking punishment for another, as the supreme moral example, and as a mediator who heals broken relationships.

Bible. This word names a collection of writings inspired by God to teach us how to live. From Old Testament stories of faithful people such as Abraham, Moses, Ruth, and David, we learn how God patiently taught humanity to be his people. The New Testament teaches us about the long-awaited Messiah—Jesus—his life, teaching, death, resurrection, and what this means for the world now and in the future.

Creation. This is a Bible word for universe. The first book, Genesis, means "beginning." It teaches that God formed the cosmos from nothing and developed it in stages concluding with the creation of humanity. God pronounced the creation good. Though damaged by evil, through the triumph of Christ over sin the cosmos will be restored. That's why Christians pray as Jesus taught them: "Your will be done on earth, as it is in heaven."

Depravity. This word names the human condition of inner sinfulness from which bad actions flow. Ever since Adam and Eve, seduced by Satan, rebelled against God, people have been marred by evil. A subtle aspect of depravity is self-deception. Fortunately, Christ's atonement includes having our hearts cleansed from this dark stain. That's why Christians use the word "gospel," it means "good news!"

Eternal life. This term encompasses both the present and the future. It conveys the enduring qualities Christ brings to believers in this life—such as peace, joy, and love. It also conveys the promise of an everlasting heavenly existence in which sin and death no longer reign, where, with new bodies, we will work with Christ to live in and care for a revitalized universe.

Faith. This word names our trust that God is, and that God rewards with salvation all who penitently call upon the Lord for salvation. Faith means we consciously decide to act upon this trust. We eagerly let our five senses become God's messengers about the world and its inhabitants. We learn to develop insights and intuitions in accordance with God's will and purposes, and to act faithfully in response to them.

God. This word names the creator-sustainer of the universe. Other terms that refer to the divine person are Lord, Yahweh, Jehovah, Allah. Using a different name doesn't add another deity. The Bible gives a trustworthy account of how God is at work in creation and in redemption. Good science explores God's book of nature to learn how to take better care of the earth and to use it for the benefit of all.

Hope. In the Bible hope refers to personal assurances about what's happening—personally, socially, and cosmically. The term indicates a believer's expectation that sin and evil won't prevail in one's own life or in the world. Divine forgiveness, redemption, and eternal life mark our expectations for the future. As the old hymn reads: "Our hope is built on nothing less than Jesus' blood and righteousness."

Incarnation. This word means "becoming flesh." It refers to how God entered our world in the person of Jesus, birthed through a specially chosen woman, Mary. God is revealed in different ways, through visions, prophets, and inward feelings. By sending Jesus as a person into our world God demonstrates love for that world and shows how we can be redeemed from sin and enabled to live as good people.

Jesus. This word names the special one born to Mary in Bethlehem, the "Son of God," who enters the human condition, becoming flesh and living among us; the Messiah predicted by the old Jewish prophets. Jesus is called the Christ, the "anointed one"—a Greek equivalent to the Hebrew term "Messiah." The followers of Jesus became known as "Christians."

Kingdom of God. A term used by Jesus to describe his vision for how people should and in God's redemptive power can relate to one another in community, bringing his values to social structures—family, society, culture, and governance. Believers seek to do this by the light of truth and the leaven of love, gathering tribes, language, ethnic groups, and nations to acknowledge that we are of one blood, created in God's image, for God's purposes.

Love. This is a very broad word! It can mean a range of attitudes and actions, including simple friendships, physical affection, and self-giving ministry. Jesus' story of the Good Samaritan illustrates this usage: a person with minority status rescues a robbery victim—a stranger—transports him to an inn, and pays for his care. Such *agape* love is modeled by Jesus, who on the cross gave himself for all of us.

Mediator. A mediator is one who brings disputing parties together. Biblically this term is used to depict how Jesus, by his life, death, and resurrection, reconciles sinful human beings to God whom they have offended by marring and soiling the highest form of his creation. By entering the human condition, and suffering with and for us, Jesus became the agent of reconciliation, drawing rebellious people back to God.

Nature. In the Bible this word is used in two ways. First, it refers to ordinary created things and their order of existence. Second, *nature* (or *natural*) refers to human beings living and acting outside the will of God, still living in a sinful state, not yet redeemed, not yet restored to union with the Creator, not yet brought into rightful relationships with other people and with creation.

Orthodoxy. This word means believing according to biblical principles as judged by the church through prayerful consensus. A companion word, *orthopraxy,* refers to "right actions." Because culture changes and influences how we frame ideas within words, orthodoxy is under constant challenge. For this reason Christian leaders test new vocabulary against biblical teachings and seek the leading of the Holy Spirit in phrasing doctrines.

Prophecy. The word means more than just predicting what's going to happen, although that is sometimes included. Basically it denotes a Spirit-anointed proclamation of God's will for a particular situation. In Bible times such messengers of God were called prophets. In the church today certain Christian leaders, either orally or in writing, may demonstrate prophetic giftedness in discerning God's will for particular circumstances.

Quaking. The Bible often refers to the physical effect of encounters with the Divine Presence—trembling, awe-stricken, crying, singing. Such emotional joy, demonstrated by folks reached for Jesus through the seventeenth-century spiritual awakening led by George Fox, led scoffers to dub them "Quakers." Ironically this nickname, given in derision, became a symbol of integrity, an alternate name for those Christians who answered Jesus' call to "be his friends and do what he taught."

Resurrection. Broadly this word denotes the restoration of the self beyond death for conscious existence in a bodily form adapted to eternal existence within a restored cosmos. Specifically, in Christian teaching the word refers to Jesus' triumph over death. By raising Jesus from the dead God offers promise and a pattern for our own continued life beyond the grave.

Salvation. This term denotes the release of penitent persons from both the guilt and the power of sin through the atoning sacrifice of Christ on the cross and by the continuing guidance of the Holy Spirit in their lives in preparation for life eternal in a restored cosmos. It marks both a decisive act of human response to the divine invitation and a continuing process of spiritual guidance throughout life.

Trinity. By this term Christian thinkers have sought to depict the threefold nature of God's revelation to us, as creator, as redeemer, as inward guide. Sometimes the formula reads: Father, Son, and Holy Spirit. The word doesn't imply three deities, but rather the ways in which the one sovereign God works in the world and in our lives. An alternate term is "triunity."

Unity. This word denotes the connectedness we feel when we acknowledge that all people are "of one blood," as brothers and sisters, equally loved by their Creator. In particular the term denotes the fellowship Christians experience with each other as they show through gospel proclamation, fellowship, and loving service what it means to live under divine governance.

Vanity. This word depicts a mind-set that focuses unduly upon things that stroke the ego, like extravagant attire or adornment of the body. It also denotes a fawning pride in one's mental or physical prowess. Vanity springs from an underlying sin of worshiping self instead of God, and of treating others as means to one's own selfish ends rather than as persons to be respected.

Worship. This word denotes the adoring response of persons to God. This response includes praise for the bounty and beauty of creation, for redemption from sin, for shared love. Worship occurs in solitude and in company of other believers, who as the body of Christ regularly celebrate redeeming grace. Worship involves not just emotions, but also proclamation of truth, whether through music, the spoken word, or silent and prayerful contemplation.

X-mas. In this contraction for Christmas, X is the first letter of the Greek word for Christ. Early Christians used it as a secret code in times of persecution. The exact date of Jesus' birth is unknown. December 25 marked the winter solstice during Roman times. In adapting to culture, Christians gave pagan celebrations enhanced meaning, showing how God offers new life to persons and to the cosmos. Some Orthodox churches celebrate Christmas on January 7.

Yuletide. Ancient European pagan people celebrated the "wheel of time" on December 25, as the days began once more to lengthen. This is another example of how Jesus' coming into the world supplanted pagan rituals and offered more than just a new year, but a new way of life. Yule logs, feasting, and gift giving gained a greater meaning.

Zion. Initially a synonym for the actual city of Jerusalem, in response to the message of Jesus the word came to mean the covenant people of God gathered into his kingdom from throughout the world. The term "Zionist" is sometimes applied to a person, Jewish or Christian, who emphasizes the Holy Land as a special physical place in God's plans. Most Christians, however, accept the more encompassing symbolic meaning of the term.

Controlling Auditory Space
in the Classroom

Despite wide availability of audio-visual aids, such as PowerPoint and printed or posted outlines, an instructor must still resort to oral speech to convey and interpret data and elicit student responses. In current culture this creates a problem: students are culturally conditioned to continuous sounds, some of it musical (generously interpreted). Television ads are swathed in psychologically persuasive lilts. So how can an instructor keep attention to extemporaneous oral communication? One could try rapid-fire rap-like rhetoric while strumming a guitar! This versatile instrument has even been used in worship to accompany pastoral prayer. (Whether this aids devotion hasn't been well researched.) Most instructors, however, cannot articulate and communicate ideas that rapidly, and they don't play guitars. So, what to do?

There are certain time-honored ways to maintain auditory control. One way is to orate with rhetorical skill, gesticulating synchronously to sustain control of the eye gate, as well as the ear gate, to student brains. But in current culture *orate* has negative connotations, i.e., pompous, stuffed-shirtish, uncool, uninflected, nasally intoned speech. Another traditional way is to fill pauses within extemporaneous address with vocalizations such as "er," "um," and "well." This is a bit old-fashioned.

Currently one achieves better rapport with young people by interjecting into one's speech phrases such as: "like," "sorta," and "you know." Some younger faculty can use such phrases as frequently as several times a minute! Presumably this keeps students from drifting out of one's auditory domain, so to speak, while one quickly ransacks one's brain for effective words to explain complex subjects.

Suppose you are explaining quantum mechanics or the theory of the leisure class. You might begin: "Now, you know, as Heisenberg, you know, and later, like, you know, Neils Bohr...." Or, "There was, like, this sociologist, you know, Thorstein Veblen, you know, a Norwegian who sorta thought...." Obviously, students *don't know*—that's why they are taking your course—but this rhetorical strategy reinforces social leveling so cherished by current culture (it is akin to removing or lowering to ground level the speaker's podium to abolish social distance).

Does this "you know" practice annoy your aesthetic sensitivity, your passion for logical progression of thought, your appreciation for rhetorical excellence? If so, there is another route to take: well-spaced, rhythmic, silent pauses accompanied by direct, compassionate eye contact. For students assaulted all their lives by promotional and background noise, silence may be just what they need to help them learn to listen to plain speech, logically organized and resonantly delivered.

Arthur O. Roberts from Podunk University,
Instructor's Manual, p. 13

Pleasant Ridge Grade School Valedictory

[Just for fun, here is my earliest formal address, written and delivered a long time ago, 1936!]

Parents, Friends and Schoolmates:

The clock of Time is swiftly ticking away the last minutes of our grade school career. Only a short period and then we shall behold ourselves as full-fledged graduates.

I do not suppose that we shall look any different after we have received our diplomas, though I wish we could. It would be wonderful if we could sprout wings and perhaps a crown and fly right off into the sky in our happiness! That, of course, is beyond the realm of reason, so the best we can hope for is to indulge in a rosy blush, a wide grin, and perhaps a stumble or two. You know how one's legs sometimes act when one feels a little bit conspicuous.

But I must hurry on to my previously indicated themes. The seconds are speeding past, they wait for no man, and I have not yet told you of the marvelous intellectual feats we accomplished in order to be seated here today. To tell the truth I defy anyone to do them justice in mere words. No one will ever know the battles we fought with mental giants, or the conquests we made in the field of education. But if we hold ourselves proudly, if there is an air of distinction about us, let me give you a hint: there is a reason! We have a right to be egotistical. We fought a hard fight—and we won.

I bring you the sincere appreciation of the class of 1936, appreciation of your interest both now and in the days that have gone. We thank you for your kindliness and helpfulness. And with these words my address will draw to a close. It is time. The last seconds have ticked themselves into oblivion, and I, as the closing representative of the graduating class, have spoken my last words. Goodbye, and good luck to you.

George Fox University Commencement 2011

"Love and Truth Working Together"

Congratulations, 2011 graduates of George Fox University! My message to you today is simply this: *Keep truth and love linked together and working as a team.* Truth takes many forms: facts, theories, deductions, principles, doctrines, metaphors, insights, intuitions. Truth is possible because the created order is reliable. Math works. So does science, artistry, and governance. Love also takes many forms: filial and conjugal affection, friendship, kindness, compassion, mercy, civility, justice. Love, too, is made possible by God's created order—and redemptive actions. In its multiple forms love enables community. When love and truth split apart bad things happen to others—and to self.

When folks try to follow truth without love, truth gets skewed into elitism and bigotry. In the name of truth heretics are hanged, apostates slaughtered, dissidents silenced. Racism and sexism mar the social landscape, scientific discoveries and inventions enrich a few but impoverish many—or they ruin rather than enhance life. Without love competition turns cutthroat, governance becomes corrupt, reputations get tarnished, the oppressed are driven to despair, or to violence. Atheistic dogmatism is bad enough, with its cynical sneering at religious faith while basking in a society blessed by its moral legacy. Religious zealotry is worse! Sanctimonious folks who blast others with harsh judgment only bring reproach upon the name of the One who told us to love neighbor as oneself. Jesus also said, "you will know the truth and the truth will set you free" (John 8:31-32 NRSV). Christians rightly proclaim that redemption liberates from sin. How subtly the mind can get snared into self-deception! Let me illustrate. With other old timers across the street at

Friendsview, I play billiards (pool). Now, the cue ball is white; the idea is to strike the cue ball with a cue stick against a striped or solid color ball and drive it into a side pocket. Every now and then one of us starts to use *another* ball *instead* of the white one. The alternate is so strategically placed the mind pretends it's white! "Oops," we say. Together we laugh at this stupid mistake. Sadly, *more significant* self-deceptions occur in the real world, often with costly results: cheating not promptly challenged, trust funds squandered, marriages ruined by infidelity, research skewed, products flawed. Probe *your* memory! Do you know what I'm talking about? I think so. Humbly let us acknowledge that we perceive truth within finite limits, and that sin subtly can warp our perception of it.

When folks try to love outside parameters of truth, love degenerates into a tangle of private preferences. Egos tussle over turf; culture sinks into a swamp of conflicting labors to stroke self-esteem. Love degenerates into lust—not just seduction or manipulation of other persons' bodies, but also their minds. Our current post-rational culture abounds with such seductions. Advertisers bypass reason to trigger assent. Promoters and propagandists would seize our ears and eyes, using sophisticated technology. Television ads display images and sounds marked by absurdity, stupidity, and violence. Music is corrupted into background patter to monopolize attention. When I was your age *legalism* was a problem—too many petty things dubbed wrong, like movie-going. Currently *permissiveness* is a problem—many moral standards treated as personal preferences. As Augustine said, rightly, the senses are God's messengers. *Let them be so!* I urge you, young friends, cherish times of silence to reduce sensory overload, to sweep away the fog of self-deception, to clear your mind from clutter, to let the Spirit guide your perceptions and choices. Heed what the apostle Paul wrote in 1 Corinthians 13, "love rejoices in the truth."

What happens when love and truth work together as a team? The common good becomes a shared goal. Governance is of the people, by the people, for the people. Commerce serves citizens well when truth and love work together. Our banking system was started in the eighteenth century by the Lloyd and Barclay families, because Quakers could be trusted to be fair and honest stewards of entrusted funds. Quakers also urged marketing at stated price, so, as one said, "a child can buy as well as an adult." No price gouging. Calvin's work ethic and Luther's insistence that all honest work is *vocation*—a calling of God—set the stage for social systems enjoyed in this and other countries. When love and truth work together freedom is maximized, and truth prospers amidst diversity.

Science and faith are once again becoming partners in truth, not antagonists, thanks to folks like Francis Collins, the scientist who headed the genome-mapping project. Impressed by the wonders of creation, *and* by the logic of morality, Collins moved from atheism to a vital Christian experience. *All* truth is ultimately revealed. The Bible is God's word written; nature is God's word through creation. When truth and love team up science serves, the arts flourish, social snobbery subsides. The Christian commitment to love neighbor as oneself continues to leaven human community. Missionaries, including George Fox alumni, bring the liberating gospel to people world-wide, *in word and deed*. They initiate projects such as bee-keeping, tree-planting, fuel-efficient stoves, sand filters for clean water. They bring improved medical and educational systems and facilities. They lift up the oppressed. In countries around the world churches bring penitent sinners into God's kingdom. Their worship bridges cultural and ethnic differences. They gather followers of Jesus into fellowships, institutions, and programs that increase their knowledge of truth in its multiple forms, and their capacity to demonstrate love in its multiple forms—interpersonally and corporately.

Everywhere youth call for justice and social equity. I commend you graduates for *your* compassionate concerns, your community and mission service stints, your witness against human trafficking and other social evils, your global perspectives. I am impressed by your disciplined acceptance of high personal moral standards. I have no doubt your career goals include concern for others, not just for self-fulfillment. Your joyous affirmation of the Christian faith warms my heart. There's lots of bad news in the world; so I conclude with a good news item, from *Christianity Today*, Direct Newsletter, March 7, 2011.

> Two weeks after President Mubarak left office, tens of thousands of Egyptians gathered in the now-famous Tahrir Square for what they called a "Friday of Cleansing and Protecting the Revolution." Right in the center of the demonstrations, Muslim Sheikh Reda Ragab and Coptic priest Father Khazman walked hand-in-hand through the square, welcomed by warm applause and cheering from protesters chanting "Muslim and Christian, we are all one." Sheikh Ragab addressed the massive crowd, saying, "We came here today to show the world that there is no sectarian strife..." And the crowd chanted in response, "The time of strife has passed."

Yes, my friends, the time for strife has passed. *Keep truth and love linked together and working as a team.* Graduates of George Fox University: *Keep truth and love linked together and working as a team!* Yes! Oh yes!

Trouble and Triumph in Anthropolis

A fable by Arthur O. Roberts [GFU alumni Homecoming, Heritage Lecture, October 26, 2012]

Truth and Love had been dwelling harmoniously in verdant Anthropolis. But one day they quarreled. The Commonwealth regents had become over-burdened. Truth had had a busy week. Staff had arrested travelers to the City who ignored speed limits, carried expired licenses, or didn't fasten seat belts. Truckers had driven past checkpoints. Errant drivers had acted nasty. Minority persons claimed harassment. Further irritants: a media commentator claimed the chief justice was a secret communist. Another denied the Holocaust. A scholar got media attention claiming the Jesus story was trumped-up fiction. A newspaper carried a story about green men in UFOs sighted in a mountain village. A television preacher claimed dinosaurs lived but a few thousand years ago.

"Why can't people follow rules, accept facts, and act sensibly?" Truth complained angrily to Love. Arresting DUIs, and coping with rule breaking, lies, hot tempers, and stupidity had been hard. Truth was tired.

Love had had a busy week. Staff had been putting out domestic and corporate fires that destroyed homes, dashed hopes for the good life, marred the social landscape, and scorched children. Folks played the blame game. "Don't lie to me—I know you've been seeing that flirty hell-cat." "So, you're the goody-goody one—hah! I heard you bully your associates." A strike having reached a stalemate, a large corporation fired five thousand workers. Anger fostered verbal venom and violence. Courts were cluttered with the mess. Legislators quibbled. It had been hard to mediate differences, to cool tempers, to prevent social chaos. Money, sex, power:

these incendiary forces sullied the realm with smog. Coping with selfishness and hate had been a chore, and Love was tired.

Nerves were raw, perspectives narrowed. So they bickered. "Why are you so picky—so legalistic?" asked Love, "why not let folks journey at speeds they feel comfortable with—it's their trip. So what if truckers are a tad overloaded, if frustrated workers drive a bit fast. Times are tough. Folks need a hand on the shoulder, not a ticket! Forget dumb road signs. Everybody knows curves can be cornered at more than forty and freeways cruised safely at eighty. Let folks determine what's appropriate and safe. Self-interest and respect for others will do the trick. Why waste time and energy on such legalistic stuff?"

"Well, they don't *all* get to the City," replied Truth, "and they sure won't unless we post route and road signs, otherwise, like today, accidents will plug the road for hours, and recklessness will send some to the morgue. Engineers know what's safe. Respect for rules demonstrates love."

"*Rigid* rules stifle maturity," huffed Love, "they hinder the flexibility that should mark behavior." "If that's the case," retorted Truth, "why not get rid of licenses of whatever sort, whether for driving cars, building houses, preparing food, practicing medicine, governing—or marrying? Is anarchy what you want? If so, get out of Anthropolis!"

"You're upset, and so am I," sighed Love. "This is my territory, too. Some regulations *are* appropriate, but as an old axiom says, 'different strokes for different folks.' Shouldn't *tolerance* be our guide? Folks must internalize respect. But, my friend, let's not quarrel. Why don't we split the Commonwealth, have separate headquarters? You deal with external stuff and I'll handle internal stuff? Then we won't fuss, okay?" So, when Truth simmered down and muttered "sure," the deal was on. Love would handle relationships. Truth would handle facts. They scanned the charter and decided it was probably okay. The territory came to be dubbed "Inner and Outer Anthropolis."

It worked pretty well, for a while. Truth got busy building safer roads, more reliable vehicles—autos, trains, airplanes, boats, motorcycles. Engineers devised protective gear of all sorts, including strap-in seats for children, even little league ball helmets. They developed machines for factory work and rigs to dig and lift all sorts of things. The pitchfork became obsolete. PowerPoint technology eliminated chalk dust (and some boring lectures). Cities became smog-free. Chemists poured talent into medical research and provided pills for physical problems suffered by man and beast—in the process providing commercial gain. ("Better living through chemistry" was an early slogan.) Medical science identified the genome, did stem cell research, and enhanced health. People lived longer. With microscopes and telescopes scientists explored the universe, and used data—from minute particles to distant galaxies—to enlighten and advance the Commonwealth.

Love got busy, too. Religious groups agreed to differ in doctrine but be kind about it, dialoguing instead of harassing each other—or hanging heretics. They organized compassionate care, ministering to persons suffering disasters, helping those who made bad choices, or were victims of abuse. Volunteers built houses for the poor. Clinics and hospitals treated sick in mind and body. Minimum wage laws were passed, and assistance provided for the unemployed and victims of hurricanes. Companies set up health and retirement plans for workers. Minorities got greater respect. Diversity enriched community. Children grew up multi-culturally. Education flourished. "Shacking up" got replaced by a more tolerant term, "relationship." Women moved more fully into the workforce, got equal opportunity to play sports. Some became leading commentators, meteorologists, pastors, and politicians. So successful was recovery from gender bias that eventually more gals than guys were earning academic degrees and entering professions.

So life in divided Anthropolis seemed to flourish. But after a time problems arose. In Outer Anthropolis scientists moved beyond external things, the hard sciences, and turned well-polished lenses upon *internal* things, the soft sciences. Philosophers quit pondering the nature of reality and focused instead on making inferences logical—verbal calculus. Mathematicians provided formulae for probabilities. This helped social planners and entrepreneurs. Sociologists probed the structure of affinity groups—family, religion, work place. Psychologists, teaming up with biologists and chemists, probed brain functions. Advertisers took note and devised ingenious ways to grab eyes and ears of folks at pre-rational levels—hawking products not on merit but by primal sensory associations.

"Truth is discovering what material is and how to use it. It's time to junk outdated universals, religious and philosophical." So some scholars pontificated. Neuroscience replaced theology. Liberated from universal principles, moral guidelines turned ruthlessly pragmatic. Ground rules only, like three strikes in baseball, became a pattern for interaction. Folks pitted self-interest against self-interest, contending over territory, power, and resources with enhanced skills and weaponry, without considering abstractions such as justice and equity. Greed destroyed community, enriching a few while impoverishing many, when self became god and selfishness a virtue. Athletes moved beyond energy drinks to enhancement drugs, arguing it was just another way to get strong, along with good food and training. If tinkering with embryos could make kids stronger, pills make people healthier, therapy tone up muscles, and technology soup up race cars, why not use chemical resources to win a game?

Such developments made both Truth and Love nervous. Would major league owners start embryonic manipulation to breed super athletes? Would universities vie for prestige by genetically modifying potential students? Would scientifically programmed aggression replace consensual, ethical cooperation? What monsters might drug lords or terrorists develop? Horrors! Such were Love's fears. Truth admitted concern but hoped *thoughtful,* pragmatic reasoning would provide adequate boundaries.

Well, Love went away mollified if not convinced, hoping altruistic feelings, even if genetically based or chemically engendered, might still support personal and social values throughout the Commonwealth. Besides, Love faced enough problems in Inner Anthropolis. Lust and debased pleasure flooded spaces created by tolerance. Youth lacked good role models. Men and women were raped; children conned into sex slavery; pornography flourished. Culture sank from seeking the good, the true, and the beautiful to wallowing in the bad, the false, and the ugly. Gossip magazines titillated readers with gross celebrity conduct. Illegal drugs flourished. On television sexual innuendos, stupid images, and noise were carefully crafted to peddle movies and merchandise. Grunge culture flourished: tattoos on arms and legs, rings in lips and tongues. Youth paid extra money for tattered jeans— "distressed" is the euphemism used. Baggy pants on guys and scraggly hairdos on gals became status symbols. Lured by "outside the box" slogans, youth got snared by manipulators, and repackaged into smaller boxes.

Without transcendent standards against which to measure values, chaos scarred the landscape: vacuous stream-of-consciousness poetry; music without melody, meter, or meaning; junk art. Values that had produced civilized culture became replaced by manipulated preferences. "See if it's right for you!" became the guide to choice. The senses, supposed to be "messengers of God" (in Augustine's classic phrase), conveying universal values, were manipulated, and wreaked havoc in the land. Virtues of temperance, prudence, hope, justice, neighborly love, and trust were replaced by vices of gluttony, anger, envy, lust, pride, and sloth. The "work ethic"—labor—a divine calling to be done with integrity, so central to what "commonwealth" implies, declined sharply. Con artists ripped off folks. Shysters pulled off pyramid schemes. Money bought political favor. Resurgent sectarian violence intensified by sophisticated technology and electronic media, brought suffering and death to thousands upon thousands, and chaos to communities. Anthropolis was rapidly losing social capital. This troubled Love greatly.

Truth became concerned about the direction language was moving. At a meeting Truth challenged Love about this. "Recently, at a conference on urban issues I listened to a lecture by a sociology professor. The guy used the phrase 'you know' 100 times in ten minutes! I counted! He also cluttered his talk with 'kinda,' 'sorta,' and 'like.' 'You know, it's kinda obvious that street violence, like...and so forth.' What rot! Jargon should not smother meaning." "Well," conceded Love, "you have a good point. But wouldn't you acknowledge that language conveys more than facts and propositions? It conveys emotional nuances. Speech is relational, helpful in acknowledging worth to listeners. Speaking had become too snobbish, elitist. Contemporary speech reinforces community; it's egalitarian. It achieves for the ear what moving a podium from platform to audience level does for the eye and...." "Well," interjected Truth, "and I suppose moving the orchestra from pit to platform reverses status?" "You know," said Love, grinning, "maybe you've got something there, let me sorta think about it. Okay? But we've got bigger problems!" They laughed, slapped hands, and acknowledged they had work to do to improve *all* of Anthropolis. So they said goodbye and agreed to meet next month.

By the next meeting things had gotten worse. Truth and Love were distraught. They grasped each other by the hand as they met at the boundary between Inner and Outer Anthropolis. "We need each other," sobbed Love. "Indeed we do," moaned Truth. So they sat on a bench by an ancient oak tree in beautiful Garden Park by the river that flows into and through the City. They sat awhile in silence, calming spirits, basking in forest beauty, watching an eagle soar, smelling fragrant flowers, feeling grass beneath their feet. Each pondered how beauty might be restored to the Commonwealth, how integrity might prevail, how order might displace chaos.

As shadows lengthened they began to converse. Truth recalled and recited lines from an ancient poet, David, "The heavens declare the glory of God and the skies proclaim the work of his hands. Day after day they pour forth speech, night after night they display knowledge." Just as Love began to cite a remembered Bible verse, "God so loved the world..." they were surprised by one who appeared on the trail beside them. The visitor was pleased. "How fortunate I am to find you!" He introduced himself. They recognized his name, a leading astronomer. "I want to tell you about the journey I have taken." He sat beside them, and continued. "For years I was an atheist, then I became an agnostic, then a theist, and now I am a Christian believer!"

Then he turned to Truth and spoke: "As I studied the universe—its enormity, its magnificence, its complexity, its intricate patterns—the words of the poem you just recited, came to me with power. I began to look beyond descriptions of things, their parts, utility—beyond material facts. A burst of intuition flooded my mind, giving coherence to what senses had discovered and reason had groped to describe. So I came to the Creator, hand over mouth, like Job of old, awe-stricken. Before the Holy One, my self-centered façade faded like fog in summer sun. I viewed the world again with *wonder*—and with greater clarity. I recalled what my old professor said: 'All truth is God's truth, and it's all revealed.' I remembered, too, what my father taught me as a child: 'The fear of the Lord is the beginning of knowledge.' Now I read nature as God's book, and find it even more fascinating than before."

Then the stranger turned to Love. "There's another part of my story. My public life is one of prestige, but my personal life's a failure. Arrogant egotism led to betrayal of marriage vows, so a year ago my wife moved out. Our daughter, Sarah, divides time between us. Recently she found a boyfriend, Jose—nice kid. They dated; he took her to church. Well, this spring she and Jose looked forward to the senior prom. About seven o'clock that evening Jose phoned, said the family car had blown a piston, could she get her dad's car? Sarah asked me, and I said sure. She quickly dressed, kissed me goodbye, got in my convertible, and drove two miles to pick up Jose. Then they hit the freeway headed for the school."

Here the scientist took a deep breath and resumed the story. "Well, she drove too fast, over eighty. Her cell phone rang and she fumbled for it (to turn it off, she claims). In doing so she swerved onto the verge. Well, the pavement edge had eroded badly and she lost control. The convertible careened down the embankment and into the river. Airbags inflated, but the water rose rapidly. She couldn't unhook her seat belt, so Jose quickly reached over and did it, yelled at her to get out. She did, and made it to shore. Jose's legs, however, were trapped by the crushed car frame, and before the rescue squad got there he had drowned."

At this point the scientist broke down. Love reached over to grip his hand. He regained composure and resumed his story. "Well, Sarah went to her mother's to heal from broken ribs and sorrow. I wondered whether Jose's family would sue. Then I thought, is that the right attitude? So I went to visit them. Jose's family welcomed me, told me what a wonderful son Jose was, how they would join him in heaven one day. They spoke of their affection for Sarah, too, and hoped she would visit. As I prepared to leave they put their arms around me, *and prayed for me!*"

The scientist sobbed a bit, then continued. "The words of an old Sunday school song came to mind, 'Jesus loves me, this I know'; there flashed before my eyes a vision of Jesus on the cross, God's supreme word about forgiving love. So I wept with Jose's parents and in their home returned to childhood faith. I am a Christian! Bible and nature both reveal divine wisdom. I hope my wife, Ruth, will forgive me so together we can help Sarah heal a broken heart."

Then the scientist stood, wiped his eyes, said "Thank you both, God bless!" then strode to the river path and disappeared. Love and Truth sat wrapped in thought. They watched the colors of the sunset fade. An owl hooted. A night creature darted across the path. Stars glowed in the darkening night. A breeze rustled leaves of the old oak tree. Love broke the silence, "Is there a sign that warns about eroded roadsides?" "Sure," replied Truth, "'Abrupt Edge,' we must post one there." "And repair the road," said Love, then added, "dividing the territory was a mistake!" "Sure was," replied Truth, "like, you know, a stupid mistake! We must be one land again." "Absolutely!" exclaimed Love. "Yes," agreed Truth, "and if we listen carefully God will teach us rightly to guide citizens toward the city." "The City of God," mused Love.

They walked down the path pondering the visitor's story. Truth thought about the way Jose's family responded so lovingly. Suddenly an idea struck: call the commonwealth to a

"Year of the Golden Rule" *Do unto others as you would have them do unto you* (Matthew 7:12). This principle should not bug secularists; over centuries many religions and philosophies have espoused this principle. We could ask officials, law guilds, health professionals, scientists, engineers, corporations, labor unions, banks, schools from kindergarten to universities, to focus *all year* on how this principle might better support both the individual and the common good. Urge scholars to document applications of the Rule. Faced by violence, drug and human trafficking, perjured officials, war, corporate corruption—and that destroyer of the civilization, anarchy—people just might rally to such a call. The "Year of the Golden Rule" could guide us toward Theopolis.

Love also pondered the visitor's story. How might human relations improve in reunited Anthropolis? Words of Jesus came to mind: "You will know the truth, and the truth will set you free" (John 8:32 NRSV). Hmm, maybe benevolence means more than handouts to the poor, common courtesies, tolerance, and piety. Maybe it includes better *knowledge* of the world, efficient use and care of the earth, need-focused medical delivery, rational management of business, transportation, and governance. Relief agencies blend science and compassion, using appropriate technology—like sand filters to provide clean water. Maybe, Love mused, we could set aside a year in Anthropolis for *everyone* to focus on how God wants truth to set folks free.

Recalling words of an ancient prophet, Love turned to Truth and quoted: "What does the Lord require of you but to do justice, and to love kindness, and to walk humbly with your God?" (Micah 6:8 NRSV). "Yes," replied Truth, "and I have an idea about putting that into practice." "Oh," said Love, "tell me about it!" "Well," replied Truth, "how about calling the whole Commonwealth to a 'Year of the Golden Rule?'" "Let's do it!" responded Love. "I've been thinking along similar lines. And we'll ask religious leaders to help curb a root problem, ego worship, by teaching individuals and groups what *walking humbly* means." "Lots of people in the realm," added Truth, "want to be just and merciful, but they feel trapped by systemic evil—economically dependent, socially conditioned to accept it. They find it difficult to follow Micah's maxim. The 'Year of the Golden Rule' might just set these captives free!"

Then, praising God, Love and Truth joined hands and walked home to wait with joy and to work with hope for the dawning of a brighter day in a reunited Commonwealth.

Visions and Dreams

Friendsview Retirement Community,
Midweek meeting, March 17, 2010

Scripture text: Acts 2:16-18 (NIV)

"This is what was spoken by the prophet Joel: 'In the last days, God says, I will pour out my Spirit on all people. Your sons and daughters will prophesy, your young men will see visions, your old men will dream dreams. Even on my servants, both men and women, I will pour out my Spirit in those days, and they will prophesy.'"

Introduction: This text describes Pentecost—that wondrous day when Jesus' disciples received the promised baptism with the Holy Spirit—and the kingdom of God was launched, cutting across cultural and linguistic barriers and enriching the world. We here today are beneficiaries of that vision as it was carried forth by faithful and discerning men and women across the centuries. The church is the witnessing community to that vision.

One of these visionary persons is Patrick. Today is Saint Patrick's Day. We honor this one who had a vision of bringing Christ to the Irish. Born in Scotland about 386, as a sixteen-year-old Roman Briton from a Christian family, Patrick was captured and sold by raiders to an Irish druid priest as a slave to tend his flock of sheep. Patrick escaped to Britain six years later, matured as a very Spirit-led Christian. God gave him a vision of returning to Ireland to evangelize the pagans who had kidnapped and enslaved him, returning good for evil like Jesus said to do. Consequently, he was commissioned by the Roman church to be an apostle to the Irish. He developed a pattern of traveling missionary-evangelists. Sometimes they worked singly, at other times in groups. Dubbed the Irish *peregrini* they evangelized Ireland, the Falkland Islands, Scotland, Germany, perhaps even Iceland. Irish monks established schools that through the dark ages preserved Christian and other manuscripts from the early centuries. There is a book, *How the Irish Saved Civilization*, by Thomas Cahill, that appeals to the pride of Irish descendants, but does support its claims that key documents of the Greco-Roman world were thus preserved for posterity. Patrick died March 17, 460—some 1650 years ago. Now the anniversary—St. Patrick's Day—is a major festival with parades and bagpipes. Shamrock festivals include wearing of the green. The shamrock is a three-leaf clover Patrick used to explain the mystery of the trinity. Sometimes a good metaphor is better than pages of theological explanation.

The hymn, "Be Thou My Vision," honors that call to faithful Christian witness. (Written in the eighth century, it was translated from old Irish into English in 1905 by Mary Byrne, music provided by Eleanor Hull a few years later.)

Be Thou my vision, O Lord of my heart;
Naught be all else to me, save that Thou art.
Thou my best thought, by day or by night,
Waking or sleeping, Thy presence my light.

Be Thou my Wisdom, Thou my true Word;
I ever with Thee, Thou with me, Lord;
Thou my great Father, I thy true son;
Thou in me dwelling, and I with Thee one.

Be Thou my battle-shield, sword for my fight,
Be Thou my dignity, Thou my delight.
Thou my soul's shelter, Thou my high tower.
Raise Thou me heavenward, O Power of my power.

Riches I heed not, nor man's empty praise,
Thou mine inheritance, now and always:
Thou and Thou only, first in my heart,
High King of heaven, my Treasure Thou art.

So much for Patrick's vision as a young person. Hear now his dreams as an old man. (From the *Confession of St. Patrick*, Christian Classics Ethereal Library, #56.)

> Behold now I commend my soul to God who is most faithful and for whom I perform my mission in obscurity...may it never befall me to be separated by my God from his people whom he has won in this most remote land. I pray God that he gives me perseverance, and that he will deign that I should be a faithful witness for his sake right up to the time of my passing.

As an old person this, too, is my dream: to be a faithful witness right up to the time of my passing. Is that your dream, too? I hope so.

What about our visions?

In 1652 George Fox, nudged by the Spirit, climbed up Pendle Hill, in England, where he had a vision of a people to be gathered to the Lord. By the end of that century, a hundred thousand people had been gathered by Fox along with some sixty young itinerant evangelists into a vibrant community of faith. Hungry seekers became redeemed finders, zealous to follow Jesus, to be part of that peaceable kingdom envisioned so long ago by the prophet Isaiah and set in motion by Jesus. My Welsh ancestors were part of that community of faith. Some of yours were, too, perhaps. As a youth under the Spirit's nudging through local Friends elders, and especially pastor Milo Ross, I entered into Fox's vision and began a preaching-teaching-writing ministry. One of my visions: that the college named after the seventeenth-century Christian reformer would become a major force for Christian witness in the world, and that Quakers worldwide would recover the vitality of that original vision.

What have been your visions? For some of you Patrick, or Martin Luther or John Calvin or John Wesley or Menno

Simons or Francis of Assisi or Roger Williams may have been the visionary whose legacy you inherited, along with those fired-up apostles at Pentecost noted in our text. Or perhaps it was a local pastor, like Milo Ross for me. Or an evangelist like Billy Graham. Or a compassionate saint like Mother Teresa. How did such historic witnesses to the wonder and power of the Holy Spirit offer you a vision for your life? And how have you passed that vision on to others?

Let's now enter into silence before the Lord. In this silence remember and contemplate in gratitude those particular visionaries, now part of the church triumphant, through whom the Holy Spirit captured *your* mind and heart years ago and guided *you* on your appointed Christian journey.

What about our dreams?

Here is one for us oldsters: that the Holy Spirit will inspire our grandchildren and others of that generation to escape the powerful clutches of cultural domination, to accept the fire of God's redeeming grace in their own lives, and then to join others of their generation to renew the Christian community of faith. To renew it both in the power of truth and in power of loving service. Dream with me that new visionaries on fire with the Holy Spirit will witness Christ's kingdom in word and deed in powerful and convincing ways. In America, all over the world. Among the poor and oppressed. Among the affluent and entrapped. Among the complacent middle class. Among persons everywhere.

Friends, some young folks *are* answering our dreams. Some by showing integrity in their jobs, whether teaching school or roofing houses. Some by faithful evangelistic witness to their friends. Others by missionary work among tribal people—translating the Bible or installing sand filters to provide clean water. Here's an inspiring—and challenging—example: In the current issue of *Mission Frontiers* (March-April, 2010) is an article by Ted Dekker and Carl Medearis entitled, "Loving Bin Laden—What Does Jesus Expect Us to Do?" These earnest Christians describe their meetings with Hezbollah and other radical Muslims, and with Israelis, with whom they pondered the words of Jesus accepted by Christians, Jews, and Muslims, "love your neighbor as yourself," and "love your enemies." Wow! What a Pentecostal vision! It may not make much difference immediately in the war-minded world, but such prophetic boldness will do more than military might in the long run to prevent a century of catastrophic war amongst contending faiths. The vision of John the Revelator inspired these courageous Christian peacemakers. John notes faithful followers of Jesus from every social affinity circle: "tribe and language and people and nation" (Revelation 5:9 NRSV). "They have conquered him by the blood of the Lamb and by the word of their testimony," writes John (Revelation 12:11 NRSV). Christ's faithful followers. "Blessed are the peacemakers," says our captain, Jesus, "for they will be called children of God" (Matthew 5:9 NRSV).

The Holy Spirit didn't close up shop after sending forth Patrick, Francis, Calvin, Luther, Menno Simons, George Fox, John Wesley, Billy Graham, and your pastoral nurturers. Pentecost continues in the hearts of George Fox students across the street, and in young folks all around the world. In faith, then, we oldsters dream of a spiritual reformation sweeping our nation and our world. Friends, it has begun. The vision of a people to be gathered to the Lord *is* being rekindled in the hearts of many youth. Thanks be to God!

Finding Joy

Friendsview Retirement Community,
Midweek meeting, May 25, 2011

What is joy?

One might define joy as

- spiritual elation, related to, but not dependent upon external circumstances;
- emotional exuberance accompanying satisfying experiences or activities;
- emotional radiance arising from peace with God.

Joy derives from God's creative, redemptive, and glorified order. Let's consider each.

Joy in the created order

Joy arises from relishing God's creation. The Psalmist wrote: "You make the gateways of the morning and the evening shout for joy" (Psalm 65:8 NRSV), and again: "The hills gird themselves with joy, the meadows clothe themselves with flocks, the valleys deck themselves with grain, they shout and sing together for joy" (Psalm 65:12-13 NRSV).

For us Friendsview folk, a walk in the canyon or a drive among St. Paul farms or across Chehalem mountain offers joy. So do resident gardens, our landscaped campus, and floral arrangements that grace the lobby and the dining hall. Thomas Merton said, "Every blade of grass is an angel singing in a shower of glory" (*Raids on the Unspeakable*, 1964, p. 196). If a blade of grass, how much more a rose? A blossoming tree? A flaming sunset? A rainbow? A frisky squirrel? A soaring bird?

Artistry is an avenue for expressing and accessing joy. For philosopher Aristotle (in *Poetics*), *art is imitation*, utilizing form, color, and rhythm. He considered it *natural* and right to delight, and to find meaning, in works of imitation. Consider landscape paintings. Framed ones hang in our hallways (I wish there were fewer eighteenth-century scenes). In our apartment we have an eastern Oregon painting by Frank Tuning, a relative of some of you, a coastal scene by the late Stan Putnam, of Portland, and paintings by an Aymara artist whose name I can't decipher. We also prize photos of visited scenic places such as New Zealand's Milford Sound. I post some on the computer screen. These honor the creation and its human caretakers. They bring joy.

Leo Tolstoy considered art *the language of emotion.* "To evoke in oneself a feeling one has once experienced and having evoked it...by...movements, lines, colors, sounds, forms expressed in words, so to transmit that feeling that others experience the same feeling—this is the activity of art." *Good* abstract art does this. Crafted objects do, too (we marvel at Divonna's quilt and Gene's carved creatures). Poetry evokes emotion. Like this one:

Five Quick Queries

Have you smelled sagebrush in the morning after rain?

How long ago did you drink water from a spring?

Your hands, what gratifying memories do they hold?

Your ears, what satisfying words have they been told?

Did you ever see an eagle on the wing?

Our Puritan ancestors, suspecting the arts of devilry, banned some for Christians, ostensibly to give God—not ego—the glory. They had a point—the arts can corrupt. As a result, however, the ugly and the mediocre got elevated over beauty and excellence. But redemption includes the restoration of the divine image in humanity *and* a right use of creation. We are to be coworkers with Christ in tending God's creation. Creative artistry is not just music like the *Messiah* or frescoes on the Sistine Chapel, or poetry that frames truth with fire, but also human-crafted things that ease burdens and delight the senses—like well-designed cars, tools, bridges, clothes, cuisine, furniture. Sanctification binds aesthetics to the work of the Holy Spirit, avoiding extremes of glitz and grunge. The senses—smell, hearing, taste, sight, and touch—are antennae for receiving God's messages. Sanctified senses discern and share God's creativity. Christ leads us back through the flaming sword into God's garden, where simplicity blends with elegance, prayer with play, and artistry with worship.

Joy in work. Doing competently any job involving created stuff brings joy. Check your memory bank for some wonderful work experiences. During our years on the Oregon coast we lived near a Job Corps, where youth learn trades. I recall how these youth would inform visitors, "I am a plumber," "I am an electrician," or, "I'm a chef." Martin Luther would be proud of them for understanding ordinary work as vocation—a call to serve others through useful labor. In 1998, I concluded a commencement address to Job Corps graduates with this poem:

> Satisfaction comes in many ways,
> in sports, good food, vacation days,
> time spent with friends, or books,
> by enhancing our, or others, looks.
> Such pleasures come and go
> Most fun provides an afterglow
> of joy, but some can leave a trail
> of tears. One pleasure never fails
> to satisfy: a job well done,
> a job well done.

What about play? An old Westminster catechism asks: "What is the chief end and duty of man?" and responds thus, "to glorify God and to *enjoy* him forever." Play is joyful, often social, activity. Play accents intrinsic over instrumental values. When we play, body, mind, and spirit unite in a way that honors creation *and* human community. I think this includes Scrabble, jig-saw and cross-word puzzles, ping-pong, and pool.

Joy in the redemptive order

A word count from the NRSV of the Bible lists 220 usages of the word *joy*. Adding cognates such as *happiness* and *pleasure* brings the number to 390. Wrote the Psalmist: "But let the righteous be joyful; let them exult before God; let them be jubilant with joy" (Psalm 68:3 NRSV).

Said Jesus: "The kingdom of heaven is like treasure hidden in a field, which someone found and hid; then in his joy he goes and sells all that he has and buys that field" (Matthew 13:44 NRSV).

Stanley Hauerwas rightly identifies God's revelation as the supreme basis for joy: "Joy is a simple willingness to live with the assurance of God's redemption." It is not some spontaneous feeling, no blithe ignoring of tragedy, not shallow optimism. "It derives from finding our true home among a people who carry the words and skills of God's kingdom of peace" (*The Peaceable Kingdom,* Notre Dame, 1983, pp. 146 ff.).

Affinity circles are all blessed by redemption: families, neighborhoods, schools, workplaces, towns, retirement homes. Examples of joy in redemption: the burden of personal sin lifted, fellowship in the family of God, smiles and hugs from loved ones and friends, occasional spiritual ecstasy, watching God redeem the lives of folks among us. Especially spiritual restoration of family members. Forgiveness is beautiful. The Amish gave the world a lesson in this a few years ago by offering forgiving love to the family of the one who had murdered several of their school children. Remember? In table devotions this morning, Ralph Beebe recalled a less-publicized story of a Quaker family who lovingly led to Christ the imprisoned rapist who had killed their daughter. North of Sheridan, and its penitentiary, the coast highway intersects a road named for that family: Payne Road. Have you seen it?

A poem, "Yeah, I'd Like That," depicts the wonder of redemptive joy. It's about a World War I veteran, maybe like my father-in-law who grumbled once: "If old men had to fight wars, they'd find other solutions."

Lord, I don't travel much anymore.
Went to the Columbia ice fields last year,
but most of the scenes I view now
are inside my head. Some are vivid,
like seeing that dirty trench near St. Lo,
the red blood spurting from my leg,
and that German boy's face—
before I blew it away. I never talk
to anyone about this, except you, Lord.
Maybe I'll meet that boy in heaven.
That would be okay. We'll recognize
and forgive each other, and maybe you
will give us constructive work to do
together, somewhere in the cosmos.
Yeah, I'd like that!

Joy in the glorified order

In heaven the Creator blends human creativity and the natural world, providing an enhanced cosmos freed from pollution and constraints of sin. As pictured in the Revelation, the New Jerusalem juxtaposes the finest of nature and human civilization—for the redeemed from every tribe, tongue, nation, and people: nature and civilization in splendid harmony. I conclude with words from *Exploring Heaven*.

Human intelligence has harnessed energies for creative enterprises that bring health to the body, delight to the mind, and joy to the spirit. Human stewards of the earth now probe inner and outer space.... They yearn to be

111

co-creators with the Divine. Purified in heaven from the curse of sin, (and adapted physically to multiple planetary systems), creative humanity will join the Master Architect in cosmic reconstruction.

What the cosmos restored in righteousness will look like materially, and how it will incorporate our earth, human artifacts, our solar system, our galaxy (and the billions of others...), we cannot say. We *can* infer that through creative application it will embody the classic longings of the heart: the good, the true, and the beautiful; and that humanity will share in shaping God's own dreams—dreams for the peaceable kingdom.

Dear friends, amid pains and aches of aging, and separation from loved ones, keep your faith fixed upon Jesus, who gives us joy; joy in the created order, joy in the redemptive order, and holds open the garden gate to joy in the glorified order.

Stormy Weather

Friendsview Retirement Community,
Midweek meeting, November 30, 2011

Hymn: "A Shelter in the Time of Storm"

Introduction: Weather is a frequent topic of conversation, especially this time of the year. Observing it and chatting about it makes us aware, indirectly, that the earth is the Lord's and that some things in life are not under our control. Coping with stormy weather reinforces our common humanity. Fascination with weather is evidenced by the many idioms we use, as this poem illustrates.

Fair Skies

Hi, Joe, thought I'd phone and shoot the breeze a bit.
Glad you called, Mac. I've been under the weather.
You're generally on cloud nine, Joe. What happened?
Well, a foggy funk hit me like a bolt out of the blue.
Mac, come rain or shine, life goes on; you'll cope.
Yeah, my friend, I will. How's your writing project?
Not so good, Joe. Hit a cold spell, I guess.
Mac, you're a good writer; fair skies await.
Words will flow; publication will be a breeze.
Joe, with my editor I can't throw caution to the wind.
Foul-weather guy, is he? Hey, Mac, I gotta run.
I'm in the garden and it's raining cats and dogs.
I'm heading for the tool shed.
Any port in a storm is it? Okay, bye, Joe!
Bye, Mac, your call brightened my day!

Beyond the power of weather to enliven language, seasonal rhythms possess metaphoric power to convey insights about life, as depicted in the following poem.

Foliage Isn't Everything

Why alders strip their leaves each fall
and stand around stiff and bare
through cold and rainy months
while conifers proudly flaunt
their lovely coats all year long
is something a botanist could elucidate
at some length, patiently ignoring
my poetic anthropomorphism.
Maybe it's all about symbiosis
in a healthy biosphere.
It looks as though some things,
and some people, apparently,
sacrifice more to common good
or just have more to give than do others.
Or does social inequity
fashion them into givers and takers?
But maybe there is more
to giving and receiving
than meets the eye:
perhaps a nexus of needs and goods
reciprocally exchanged?
Or losses that redemptively
mulch the soil for growth?
In folks as well as forests
foliage isn't everything.

(from *Let the Spirit Soar)*

Scripture: Matthew 14:22-36 (NIV) This episode in Jesus'
ministry followed the feeding of the five thousand:

Jesus made the disciples get into the boat and go on ahead
of him to the other side, while he dismissed the crowd.
After he had dismissed them, he went up on a mountain-
side by himself to pray. Later that night, he was there

alone, and the boat was already a considerable distance from land, buffeted by the waves because the wind was against it. Shortly before dawn Jesus went out to them, walking on the lake. When the disciples saw him walking on the lake, they were terrified. "It's a ghost," they said, and cried out in fear. But Jesus immediately said to them: "Take courage! It is I. Don't be afraid." "Lord, if it's you," Peter replied, "tell me to come to you on the water." "Come," he said. Then Peter got down out of the boat, walked on the water and came toward Jesus. But when he saw the wind, he was afraid and, beginning to sink, cried out, "Lord, save me!" Immediately Jesus reached out his hand and caught him. "You of little faith," he said, "why did you doubt?" And when they climbed into the boat, the wind died down. Then those who were in the boat worshiped him, saying, "Truly you are the Son of God." When they had crossed over, they landed at Gennesaret. And when the men of that place recognized Jesus, they sent word to all the surrounding country. People brought all their sick to him and begged him to let the sick just touch the edge of his cloak, and all who touched it were healed.

I don't know what *outer* storms you may have encountered. Our family experienced the Columbus Day storm of 1962. Remember it? I recall speeding down Rex hill while trees twisted and fell. Upon reaching our Springbrook home our family fled to the basement just before an oak tree crashed into the living room. Whew! We were scared, and grateful to be alive!

I don't know what *inward* storms you may have encountered over the years and how you coped. But *you* recall them! Your response was probably somewhat like good old Simon Peter: faltering faith crying out for a helping hand from Jesus. Reflect upon those storms for a bit and breathe a prayer of praise to God that you weathered them. And became stronger for it.

We oldsters experience stormy weather emotionally. I remember George Thomas saying that "being old isn't easy." In the winter, days are short but the hours seem long. For us the climate might suitably be dubbed "heavy weather"—not just physically achy days and sleepless nights but emotional cold spells lacking the warm glow of spiritual ecstasy; icy winds of anxiety over many things: health, frailty, loneliness, lack of productivity, family members straying from the faith. We oldsters experience gales of grief over loss of loved ones. We miss the warmth of grandkids who years ago sat on our laps while we read stories to them, but who are now scattered around the world, busy adults, with their own families and affinity circles.

Thankfully, throughout the stormy times of our life, ghosts of the past did not terrorize us, the waves of hard circumstances did not swamp our boats, for we heard Jesus' voice bidding us to come. And we obeyed. Were we fearful? At times, yes, but we reached out and grasped his hand. So, dear friends, on our lake of life here at Friendsview, buffeted by waves of doubt or depression, under various sorts of heavy weather, we can more tightly grasp his hand. I close my message with this prayer poem:

"Lord Save Me!"

Jesus, how gently you chide my lack of faith
when I flounder and begin to sink:
oh, no, *I* cannot walk on water!
How lovingly, my Lord, you grasp my hand
and haul me up onto the boat
to waiting friends. You calmed the storm!
I trust you, Jesus. I will follow you,
however wild the weather
on the lake, or in my heart.
Yes! Oh, yes I will!

How the Kingdom of God Flourishes

Friendsview Retirement Community,
Midweek meeting, January 2, 2013

Hymn: "We've a Story to Tell to the Nations"

At midweek meeting five years ago I spoke on a Christmas theme, recognizing that some world Christians celebrate Jesus' birth on January 7. Today, however, the focus is on the impact of God's gift upon humanity. Call the message "How the Kingdom of God Flourishes." Yes, there's much evil in the world: infidelity of public leaders, mass murder, theft, enslavement, and abuse of power. Evil dominates the news. Scandal sells. Television ads picturing stupidity and destruction grab our eyes and ears. The December 21 doomsday scare is over. So let's focus on good news. Scripture offers guiding words.

Scripture: Ponder Jesus' parables of mustard seed and yeast (Matthew 13:31-33 NIV):

> He told them another parable: "The kingdom of heaven is like a mustard seed, which a man took and planted in his field. Though it is the smallest of all seeds, yet when it grows, it is the largest of garden plants and becomes a tree, so that the birds come and perch in its branches."

> He told them still another parable: "The kingdom of heaven is like yeast that a woman took and mixed into about sixty pounds of flour until it worked all through the dough."

The Mustard Seed parable shows how God's kingdom grows in the garden of the world. First, picture that seed as a small group of men and women living in a corner of a pagan empire, who, inspired by the resurrected Christ and empowered by the Holy Spirit, faithfully proclaimed the gospel. Then ponder how through two thousand plus years the world has been blessed as folks came to Christ. The disciple Mark went to Egypt, Thomas to India, Andrew to Slavic peoples. From a cluster of congregations gathered to Christ by Paul and associates, churches in what are now called Greece, Turkey, Italy, France, Germany, Russia, and other European nations, grew and flourished. Over time a Christianized Europe arose from shambles of the Roman Empire. In the fifth century a released Christian slave, Patrick, returned to native Ireland to preach Christ; his zealous missioners evangelized Britain. Several centuries later, European Christian émigrés shaped the course of history in North America. Scholarly followers of Jesus such as Roger Williams, William Penn, and Jonathan Edwards gave kingdom direction to a new nation, whose goal was to offer "liberty and justice for all." We are heirs of that legacy.

A seventh-century Persian Christian, Alôpen, trekked the Silk Road to China to share the gospel, welcomed by a benign ruler. This Asian witness, interrupted by hostile regimes, resumed in later centuries through ministry of missionaries from Europe and America. After decades of repression, since 1980 phenomenal growth has occurred. (Currently there are about 100 million Christians in China.) The world's largest Christian congregation is in South Korea, the Yoido Full Gospel Church, with nearly a million members organized into an expanding circle of cell groups. In recent centuries, African and Latin American nations were evangelized by thousands of missionaries. There are now more Quakers in Africa than in Europe and North America, more in Bolivia than in England. Other Christian groups could report similar data.

That small group who witnessed the risen Lord took seriously his command to "tell Jesus' story to the nations." So have their followers. John the Revelator (Revelation 7) envisioned a multitude, "from every nation, tribe, people and language," standing before the throne and before the Lamb. It's happening right before our eyes! The Bible has been translated into nearly three thousand languages; Wycliffe people are working on remaining minority ones. The tiny mustard seed has grown into a tree with branches spreading globally. Currently there are more than two billion Christians, a third of the world's people. Yes, growth has been marred. Gospel treasure is held in earthen vessels. Christians too often have been ignorant, misguided, or arrogant. Sometimes they slaughtered each other over issues of power, territory, or theology. Often they got trapped in social systems that hinder good and foster evil. Sometimes subtle anti-Christian culture snares believers. Evil continues to wreak havoc. But that's another story. On January 2, 2013, in the words of the hymn we sang, we celebrate God's great "kingdom of love and light."

Leaven. Consider some ways the gospel has enriched the world. Jesus' second parable depicts how nations have been impacted by God's kingdom through the testimony and actions of Jesus' followers who take seriously his call to be in the world but not of it. Yeast works in different kinds of dough. Bread (like people groups) varies in form: rye bread, raisin bread, wheat bread. Some are tastier, some more nourishing. Bread has been dubbed the staff of life. Breaking bread together signifies human community. The action of yeast is so much part of our diet we don't give it much thought. Scientists can explain its chemistry. I'm content to use Jesus' imagery to illustrate how kingdom faithfulness makes the social order morally, spiritually, and aesthetically palatable and nourishing, how God's kingdom leavens that global loaf we call civilization. Like salt, as Jesus said, his followers give flavor to life. Biblical justice and mercy have blessed the world.

Consider how the gospel permeated a collapsing empire, as Jesus, not Caesar, became honored as Lord, and how this leavening brought vitality as tribes segued into nations. Scholars such as Augustine and Aquinas—and rulers like Charlemagne—discerned that all truth is God's truth, and education flourished. A monotheistic understanding of an orderly creation laid a foundation for science and for the arts. The concept of "commonwealth" displaced autocracy and plutocracy in many countries. Luther proclaimed the "priesthood of believers"—every Christian a minister to neighbor—and ministry multiplied. Calvin taught that *all* labor, whether with tools, words, or notes is a vocation—a calling from God. Such faithful stewardship honors the creation, aids governance, supports commerce, provides health care, and enriches culture. Christian insights about work and ministry have blessed the world, giving dignity and economic stability to ordinary folks. Guided by biblical principles, our government affirms "inalienable rights": life, liberty, and pursuit of happiness (Declaration of Independence). Along with other countries, America has been richly blessed by gospel leaven.

The Quaker demonstration of ethical integrity in business fostered a banking system that has benefited the world. In the nineteenth century, John Bright, a member of the British Parliament, inaugurated the secret ballot and joined an American brother in Christ, John Woolman, to put their nations on paths toward abolishing slavery. Think how far our country has moved, by applying kingdom ethics, to affirm the dignity of all persons. While pastor of a church in Kansas City in 1950, I was booed at a community gathering when I affirmed the right of a black couple to buy a home in our neighborhood, and told assembled folks I visited them and found them to be fine folks. When you were children could you have envisioned a person of color serving as our president? Or a woman as secretary of state? Or as church superintendent? Rejoice in compassionate care organizations founded and sustained by Christians, such as Habitat for Humanity, Heifer International, the Mennonite Central Committee—and many others. Christian leaven works its power in deeds of love and through words of truth.

Christians leaven the socio-political order. We don't always agree with political policies, but patiently we work for kingdom principles: justice, mercy, and integrity. Freedom keeps nations open to gospel leavening, although persecutions can strengthen Christian witness and lead to penitent renewal. (This is happening in Africa.) Christians try to be loyal citizens even if some policies and actions fall short of biblical standards. As loyal opposition we pay taxes even if government sanctions conduct we deem wrong (for example, for me, capital punishment, the Iraq war, same sex marriage). We can't segment morality: one ethic for government, one for corporations, and one for individuals. *But we let the leaven work!* Sometimes options seem limited to choosing a lesser evil, what Bonhoeffer, during World War II, dubbed "tragic moral choice." We trust kingdom leaven to be active despite deficient or partial human applications.

Paul wrote to Christians of Colossae "the gospel is bearing fruit and growing throughout the whole world" (Colossians 1:6 NIV). If then, how much more now! Truth and love leaven the world. Stakes are getting higher. Technology ramps up options for both good and evil, offering solar panels and smart bombs. Our world may face heightened violence, ecological disasters, and possibly nuclear war. Whatever comes, "we've a story to tell to the nations." Patiently, by word and deed, we proclaim the "kingdom *of love and light*," trusting that at *God's timing* the Lamb will complete the victory.

Let us now engage in silent prayer on three topics:

1. Christians under persecution.

2. Our president and Congress, that they will rise to honorable cooperation.

3. Our children and grandchildren, that they will not only relish the fruits of Christian witness but will also nourish the roots.

Weeds

Friendsview Retirement Community,
Midweek meeting August 14, 2013

Hymn: "Jesus Calls Us"

Scripture: Matthew 13:24-29, 36-39 (NIV)

Jesus told them another parable: "The kingdom of heaven is like a man who sowed good seed in his field. But while everyone was sleeping, his enemy came and sowed weeds among the wheat, and went away. When the wheat sprouted and formed heads, then the weeds also appeared. The owner's servants came to him and said, 'Sir, didn't you sow good seed in your field? Where then did the weeds come from?' 'An enemy did this,' he replied. The servants asked him, 'Do you want us to go and pull them up?' 'No,' he answered, 'because while you are pulling the weeds, you may uproot the wheat with them....' The one who sowed the good seed is the Son of Man. The field is the world, and the good seed stands for the people of the kingdom. The weeds are the people of the evil one, and the enemy who sows them is the devil. The harvest is the end of the age, and the harvesters are angels."

Darnel

These weeds (tares) in Jesus' parable were darnel, a type of ryegrass that early on resembles wheat stalks. Our Scripture alerts us to the presence of false kingdom plantings but warns us that certain efforts to destroy such weeds can damage God's kingdom crop—believers.

In our efforts to sustain people of the kingdom—and their values—we must acknowledge and accede to a *continuing* social mix of good and evil in corporate life. Implications? No crusades against other religions, no hanging of heretics (literally or figuratively), no racial or gender harassment, no denying civil rights to persons of secular or alien ideologies, no demands for special civic favors for Christians, no demeaning "less enlightened folks." Trying to uproot folks deemed tares in God's field puts good Christians at peril. Remember, the growing season isn't over! Let's work and pray that kingdom wheat does not get uprooted by misplaced zeal to eradicate certain social evils. In the cause of kingdom values it is better to endure pain than to inflict it. In many ways a democracy is a Christian-influenced corporate affirmation of how best to cope with a social mix of good and evil. Are we content to trust Jesus, to forego hostile attitudes, to await judgment time, to let angels be the harvesters? Remember, God is the final judge of thoughts and intents of the heart!

Morning Glory

Scripture: 1 Timothy 6:9-10; 1 Thessalonians 5:23-24 (NIV)

Those who want to get rich fall into temptation and a trap and into many foolish and harmful desires that plunge people into ruin and destruction. For the love of money is a root of all kinds of evil. Some people, eager for money, have wandered from the faith and pierced themselves with many griefs.

May God himself, the God of peace, sanctify you through and through. May your whole spirit, soul and body be kept blameless at the coming of our Lord Jesus Christ. The one who calls you is faithful, and he will do it.

Morning glories are climbers with slender stems, heart-shaped leaves, and trumpet-shaped flowers. Plants grow rapidly, and self-seed easily. Their colorful flowers attract butterflies and hummingbirds. Seeds are highly toxic if ingested. By their ability to crowd out other plants, morning glory merits the term "invasive species." I discovered this the hard way. When we moved into a house many years ago I decided to turn the back yard into a lawn. Weeds covering the neglected area included morning glory. Well, I roto-tilled the yard, raked it, and planted grass. Alas, every chopped-up bit of morning glory grew!

What is the lesson? Pride, manifested in lust for *power, possessions, position,* or *prestige,* proliferates if not purged. Covering it up just brings grief. I testify to the subtle force of this. So, I expect, can you. The biblical term for such purging of pride is *sanctification.* Given the current culture of self-fulfillment this is a difficult and neglected, but important doctrine. Paul's admonition to let the "God of peace sanctify you through and through" remains valid. To let the Spirit purge pride and self-esteem is a vital part of conversion. "Dying out to self" isn't easy; but it is wonderful when experienced, and the results in our lives—body, soul, and spirit—are more beautiful than egocentric lawns infested with pride—however profitable or psychologically fulfilling.

Canada thistle

Canada thistle merits the appellation "thorn" as used in Jesus' parable of the soils ("Other seed fell among *thorns,* which grew up and choked the plants, so that they did not bear grain"). This prickly perennial infests crops, pastures, and disturbed soils. Farm kids were sometimes sent to dig thistles from the cornfield—earning a bit of spending money. Cattle avoid thistles and pasture infested by this spiky pest.

What thorns choke out Christian plantings? Jesus tells us: "life's *worries, riches,* and *pleasures*" (Luke 8:7-8, 14 NIV). For me the most thorn-like temptation has been worry. Oh, yes, good seed got threatened by my naughty youthful pleasures—like dumping rotten apples on a neighbor's beautiful lawn—and by more serious infidelities. (Make your own list, and, with me, praise God for forgiving grace!) As a mature adult, scholarly ministry seemed more important than accruing wealth. Finances somehow got attended to in a context of prudent living and generous giving.

But I'm good at fretting! (I admit having gone to hospital needlessly, and having had anxiety attacks.) A fertile imagination may create poetry, give lectures, and write books. But it can also make one overly critical of others—and quite skilled in self-deception—endangering gospel plantings and inducing dry spirituality. Hmm, thistles in an old man's garden! A preventive discipline is prayer. Especially at night. And joyfully receiving the Lord's showers of blessing. Are worries, riches, or pleasures choking God's good seed in the garden of your heart? Pray about it now.

Dandelion

Some people consider the dandelion a pesky weed that needs to be pulled from the lawn, or sprayed along the sidewalk. Herbalists consider it a source of vitamins and minerals. Native Americans, among others, used dandelion for medical purposes. With others I consider it a pretty flower to be enjoyed.

Let the dandelion symbolize the abundant life Jesus promises believers: "I have come that they may have life, and have it to the full!" (John 10:10 NIV). Unlike pesky thistles or morning glory, the dandelion doesn't crowd out good seedlings. Christians have struggled to fulfill Jesus' teaching—to be in the world but not of it. Puritans revolted against Victorian snobbish superfluity. Amish took a rigorously separatist stance. Second-generation Quakers avoided worldliness by banning drama and instrumental music and by wearing plain, unadorned, gray garb. (Margaret Fox, who loved the red cloth George had brought her from America, dubbed this "a silly gospel.") Mostly, however, the church has opted for a *guarded environment* and has sought to delineate boundaries between good and evil in sensory delights.

My youth was shaped by a guarded environment. Certain things were taboo: movies, dancing, pool playing, alcohol, tobacco, playing cards. "Be modest, dress up for church," was a mostly unwritten code. Church provided aesthetics: music, parties, artistry, sports. 4-H clubs and church schools offered culturally enriching programs and activities.

Over time, however, this stance became legalistic—a little jingle jibed: "when you're saved you don't attend movies; when you're sanctified you don't watch them on television." Metaphorically speaking, in trying to avoid worldliness— dandelions got pulled out. Current *coziness* with worldly culture cautions us, however, to be concerned about *invasive* plants that *do* threaten Christian faithfulness (especially for younger people—the ryegrass, the thistles, the morning glory, and other invasive plants infesting God's kingdom). But enjoy, and be blessed by, the dandelions, the daisies, and other flowers that beautify our roadsides—literally and figuratively. So relax with a cup of coffee, and enjoy the Saturday night movie, a good novel, an art exhibit, attractive clothes, a tasty dessert, a concert in Bauman auditorium; or join me in a game of pool some afternoon! "All things bright and beautiful, the Lord God made them all."

Pondering Paradigm Shifts in Certain Biblical Models

Altar

A central biblical theme is *sacrifice*. Picture a lamb slain at a stone altar to atone for sins in an ancient tribal society. Fast forward to the nineteenth century. Picture Iowa Quaker farmers, moved by passionate preaching, penitently weeping at revival benches, dying out to sinful self in gratitude to the Jesus, the sacrificial Lamb of God.

Tabernacle

A central biblical theme is *covenant*. Picture a close ethnic group, mobile, searching for a God-blessed homeland offering sustenance and security, worshiping in a portable, but richly symbolic tent. Fast forward to the late nineteenth and early twentieth century. Picture Quaker farm families trekking to the American West, seeking their "land of milk and honey," where in close-knit communities, worshiping in modest meetinghouses with altar rails, they shielded families against worldly onslaughts, and through word and deed witnessed Christ's redemptive power.

Temple

A central biblical theme is *glory*. Picture this covenant group comfortably ensconced in a fruitful homeland, grateful for social stability, worshiping with ceremonial ritual in a beautiful building. Fast forward to mid twentieth century. Picture Quakers now comfortably, and prosperously, enmeshed within a stable, urbanized culture enriched by Christian values (although subtly tainted by egocentricity) blending the good, the true, and the beautiful in their culture and artifacts.

Synagogue

A central biblical theme is *wisdom*. Picture leaders of this group, concerned about diminished faith within a stable society, finding ways to teach moral law and spiritual disciplines based upon divine revelation. Fast forward to late twentieth century. Picture Quakers struggling against surging secularism, seeking through programs of Christian nurture for children and adults a biblical middle ground between legalism and antinomianism. See their schools impart a Christian worldview as well as excellent vocational education to thousands of students.

Upper Room

A central biblical theme is *power*. Picture leaders of this group, anointed by the risen Christ, recovering the vision of a people through whom all nations will be blessed, and devoting their lives to this mission. Fast forward to the twenty-first century. Picture Quakers in a restless, revolutionary age, blessed and cursed by technologies having power either to enhance or to destroy group identities—and human solidarity. See them trying to persuade without manipulating, to find ways to keep truth and love linked together and working as a team. See them humbly praying for a fresh, enabling, Pentecostal anointing.

(Northwest Yearly Meeting pastors network
December 28, 2011)

Christmas 2011

Dear family and friends,

We celebrate with you the *first* act of the central real-life drama of the cosmos—at least for our part of it—the coming of Jesus, the Christ. (How divine drama plays in the other four trillion planets in our galaxy, and elsewhere, remains a mystery; maybe one day we will know.)

Consider the stage: Palestine. Why this place? Here lived folks who for centuries had worshiped God, the Creator, who taught them how to live, and promised through them a Messiah who would revolutionize the world. The Old Testament recounts their stories.

Consider two lead players: Mary, whom God chose to bear this special divine-human person, facing scandal, hostility, and a foreboding of sorrow, and fiancé Joseph, who faces ridicule for taking God seriously. How God trusted and honored these faithful young people!

Consider the cast: joyous folks who got God's message: shepherds; devout oldsters like Simeon and Anna; and a party of Persian scholar-rulers (magistrates), guided by a star, riding camels a thousand miles to honor baby Jesus in a manger. Add animals and an angel choir.

Then there were the hostile ones: religious leaders so eager to protect privilege and pet notions they couldn't grasp what God was doing; political leaders, like Herod, fearing loss of status and political support.

The New Testament narrates the full story of God's gift to the world: Jesus, whose life, sacrificial death, and resurrection triumphs over evil. History reveals Jesus' power to transform human life and the social order. How blessed we are because of God's great gift!

In celebrating the drama of Christ's birth this year we are joined by two billion other folks around the globe (including now one hundred million Christians in China).

Best of all, we are joined by family and friends who, as followers of Jesus, demonstrate a passion for truth and a commitment for love in a sometimes hostile or indifferent world.

We are maintaining health, although strength ebbs. Our walks are shorter, naps longer. Friendsview Retirement Community is a good place: loving care, nourishing food, supportive friendships. Attendance at academic, cultural, and athletic events street at George Fox University less frequent. We enjoy drives among forest and farmland. This fall gold and red foliage seemed unusually beautiful—but then we say that every year! A family picnic in July was a wonderful occasion. We are blessed by family visits—children, grandchildren, great-grandchildren, and by their phone calls and correspondence. And many pictures!

Lots of love, Arthur and Fern Roberts

Seventieth Wedding Anniversary

November 7, 2013, was our seventieth wedding anniversary. Most of our family came for a celebration dinner at our Friendsview home on Saturday the 9th. It was a fun time, full of hugs, family stories, and looking at old wedding pictures. And watching great-grandchildren run and play.

Addendum

Transitions (Momentous or Otherwise) over Sixty Years

Fern and Arthur Roberts 2003

1. From wing-tip Florsheims to Hush Puppies
   to New Balance tennis shoes;
   from green double-breasted suits,
   to tweeds, to navy blue basket weave,
   to Icelandic sweater and slacks.
   From girdle to garter belt to panty hose,
   spike heel to flats to New Balance walking shoes;
   from suits to Icelandic sweaters and slacks.

2. From Campbell's oxtail soup from the can
   to home cooked ham and bean soup;
   from ice cream cones to peanut butter malts
   to apples and cranberries and yogurt.

3. From lawn bowling to tennis to swimming to golf;
   from Rook to crossword puzzles and Scrabble.

4. From wood stove to electric furnace to gas stove
   to wood stove and electric baseboard radiator.

5. From apartment to rental house to parsonage
   to vet house to old house to new house to coast house.

6. From hunting through pockets for nickels for ice cream cones
   to pondering the best investments.

7. From Walt Disney films (101 Dalmatians)
   to foreign films at Cinema 21, to VCR movies,
   to rereading Hardy, Greene, and Steinbeck.

8. From treating the children to ice cream
   after Wednesday night prayer meeting
   to sending grandchildren to Twin Rocks camp.

9. From taking the children to Fogarty Beach
   to having the grandchildren in our Yachats beach home.

10. From shopping for clothes and books in Portland
    to ordering them from L. L. Bean and Harper.

11. From King James Version to Good News Bible
    to New International Version.

12. From book condensations
    to classics.

13. From packing box furniture
    to store bought stuff and custom built black walnut furniture.

14. From Arthur's customized clocks
    to Arthur's customized clocks.

15. From Arthur's customized clocks
    to customized putters and walking sticks.

16. From scrambling over the rocks on the beach
    to walking through the village.

17. From eating at home mostly
    to eating out mostly, especially
    Fridays at Izzies for clam chowder.

18. From reading to our grandchildren
    to writing to them, and
    taking them to dinner when they visit.

19. From playing golf before breakfast
    to playing golf in mid-day when it's warmer.

20. From Arthur's writing
    to more of Arthur's writing.

21. From Fern's quilting
    to more of Fern's quilting.

22. From taking vitamins
    to taking more supplements.

23. From belts
    to suspenders or stretchable pants.

24. From strong love
    to a stronger love for each other.

25. From faith in God
    to a deeper faith in God.

Events of Varying Importance in the Roberts' First Sixty Years of Marriage, 1943-2003

On November 8-10, 1943, the weather on the Oregon beach was sunny and warm, and the Dorchester House a posh coastal resort for our honeymoon.Fifty years later the Dorchester became a retirement home.

On a June day of 1944 an elder of the Everett Friends Church took one look at the newly arrived pastors and exclaimed, "Why you are just children!"

One glorious day in 1945 the Roberts and the Willcuts explored Flapjack Lakes in the Olympics. The hike made them so famished they ate all the packed lunch, forgetting the dog Butch. We encountered a nest of hornets, which perversely, stung hungry Butch the worst. And on a cable car bridge Arthur let the mechanism slip and it ran over Fern's finger. The best of times, the worst of times.

In 1946 we mulched the weeds in the back yard to make a lawn of our new rental house, only to discover a few weeks later that every little chunk of the morning glory vines sprouted and flourished. Fortunately the baby, Lloyd, flourished with more conventional singularity.

In 1947 we put red bumper guides on the new battleship grey Chevrolet.

In 1948 the Roberts' dog, Butch, bit another postal delivery man and was himself, soon afterward, alas, dispatched. The Roberts soon departed to Kansas City.

In 1949 we went ice sledding in Swope Park, Kansas City, Missouri. Maybe Ed and Betty Roberts were there.

In 1950, while attending seminary in Kansas City, Arthur became a salesperson for a local Chrysler agency, but after he sold one car the corporation was shut down by an extended strike.

In 1951 Fern left the Columbia Tank office building by a second story window ahead of the flooding Missouri River. A few months later we fled for New Hampshire.

One December day in 1952 Stubby the Cat, a bonus gift for buying a gallon of maple syrup, sulked behind the stove because he was jealous of the newly arrived twins, Patricia Mae and Teresa Mae.

In 1953 we precipitated a minor celebration at Yellowstone Park—the first car with a New Hampshire license that season—enroute to Newberg, with Lloyd, Patricia, and Teresa, and most of our earthly belongings in or on the 1951 Studebaker Commander.

In 1954, to make ends meet, the Roberts moved into vet housing (dorm parents) on the GFC campus.

In 1955 we jazzed up our vet house by parking a new Mercury Montclair beside it.

In 1956 Fern made a jacket for Arthur and a skirt for herself from Scottish wool plaid. [AOR still wears his]

In 1957 Patricia, who had learned to whistle, began accompanying hymn singing in church.

In 1958 Stan Thornburg tangled head on with a fly trap at our old Springbrook place; it took Fern a long time to clean him up.

In 1959 Lloyd won a purple ribbon for his sheep at the fair.

In 1960 Patti broke her collarbone doing somersaults in the living room.

In 1961 Dean Gregory, Friends superintendent, wrote urging us not to be discouraged by criticism.

On Columbus Day 1962 the wind got so strong we fled to the basement, just before an oak tree crashed into the living room.

In 1963 we grafted Brooks prune scion wood onto trees that were flattened by that Columbus Day storm.

In 1964 Arthur ran for Oregon State Representative and was defeated.

During his navy term (1964-8), after considerable prodding, Lloyd wrote us sixteen letters, in most of which he asked "How are Sally and the cats?"

In 1965 we landscaped around our new house and put a ping-pong table in the recreation room.

In 1966 Teri broke her toe at Fogarty Beach. Emergency hospital charges came to $43.25.

In 1967 during a psychedelic show at the state fair Teri passed out and was sent to the hospital.

In 1968, under social pressure, Arthur shaved his beard for Commencement. When Patti and Teri noticed this a few days later they bemoaned its loss. The beard was restored and has remained ever since.

In 1970 Arthur's picture, snapped during a New York visit, appeared in a fifth-grade textbook illustrating immigrant diversity. He was wearing a beret.

In the summer of 1971, Fern and I camped in the wilderness. After a cramped sleep in the back of the SAAB we took a bracing swim in a nearby stream, only to discover the place wasn't as isolated as imagined. Our grandparent era began that year with the birth of Robin Roberts.

In 1972 Arthur quit being dean of the faculty;
Fern was grateful.

In 1973 the girls accompanied us on a Quaker gathering/
sightseeing trip to New Zealand and Australia.
They flew home early; after Fiji and Sidney,
discussion groups seemed pretty dull.

In 1974 Fern suffered a pancreatitis attack. It was hard
to convince the doctor she wasn't abusing alcohol,
which was the only humorous aspect of an otherwise
difficult time.

In 1975 Fern wrote Arthur, away on a professional journey,
a very loving poem, with a summary line, "I miss
you in so many ways." It was much shorter than
the one Arthur had written her, partly because
it did not contain lines such as "I love you
because you prepare breakfast."

In July 4, 1976, Sunday our SAAB collapsed somewhere in
Canada; the only mechanic we could find couldn't
speak English but after five hours he fixed the car.

We celebrated Christmas of 1977 in the Philippines,
and first saw Patricia's baby girl, April Nielsen.
Teresa's baby girl, Heidi Rogers, born that same
spring, lived closer to us.

In 1978 we visited our Eskimo friends, and welcomed
the birth of Sarah Roberts to Lloyd and Cheryl.

In 1979 we enjoyed a conference in Gwatt, Switzerland,
but in Zurich we could not afford dinner.

In 1980 Lloyd convinced us to buy a Honda. Seth Roberts
and I took a ride in it and had milkshakes.

In 1981 a nun said we were an answer to her prayer for
buying her house in Yachats. That year we also
led a GFC tour group to China. Our tour guide,
Shu-Guo, later came to the college, became a
Christian, and now lives in North Carolina
with her husband and two daughters.

In 1982 they gave a party for Fern when she retired
from 22 years teaching at Boise Elementary
in Portland, Oregon.

In 1983 we sold the house the nun had sold us.
We took the buyers to lunch.

In 1984 Fern hit an errant truck broadside and learned
that seat belts do save lives although they make
purple stripes on the body. The Honda was totaled,
but not Fern. Lucky gal!

In 1985, with the help of Teri and John, maple boards from
Arlington high school gym became the floor of our
new Yachats house. Fern went to Hawaii to witness
Laura Nielsen's birth.

In 1986 Arthur again gave the faculty lecture. Thirty years
before he had used 116 footnotes to discuss "the
meaning of judgment in history." This time he used
pictures and poems to depict the automobile as icon.
A better response!

At the end of the calendar year 1987 Arthur completed
his full time teaching at George Fox College.

On January 1, 1988, we moved to Yachats from the
Springbrook house, our home for a quarter century.

In 1989 we worshiped in Moscow, Russia. One old woman
hugged Fern and together they wept in the joy of
Christian fellowship. We stuffed the offering plates
with hundreds of rubles.

In 1990 we visited Iceland just to see the land of fire and ice. At home we saw John David hit home runs.

Sister Marjorie succumbed after a long struggle with Alzheimers.

In 1991 we dined at The Golden Angel, Steenwijk, Holland, from which grandfather Jansonius embarked to the New World in 1873.

In 1992 accompanied by Lloyd and Cheryl, we visited seventeenth century ancestral homes in Wales.

In 1993 we watched Heidi and Sarah play volleyball. The autobiographical *Drawn by the Light* was published.

In 1994 Robin and her grandpa did research together for the book, *Messengers of God*.

In 1995 Fern received a hip transplant.

In the fall of 1996 Arthur was elected Mayor of Yachats, as a write-in candidate, by one vote, and the win held up under legal challenge. Fern started quilting with other ladies. *Messengers of God* was published.

In 1997 we went to Kotzebue to help Eskimo Quakers and others celebrate the 100th anniversary of the coming of Christianity. We bought our fifth Honda Accord.

In 1998 Arthur was re-elected mayor of Yachats, by a two-thirds majority.

In 1999 we began to be regulars at Izzy's in Newport on Fridays, especially enjoying the clam chowder.

In 2000 Fern started feeding and making friends with the crows. She also kept active on a prayer chain for human friends. Arthur kept on making walking sticks and clocks, and mentoring graduate students.

On January 1, 2001 Arthur retired from being Mayor, and also from editing *Quaker Religious Thought* but didn't stop writing. We began to socialize with neighbors over morning muffins at Robin's Coffee Shop. Heidi received her master's degree in teaching at GFU. Brother-in-law Ivan Adams died.

In 2002 the "County Road 804S right of way" issue was settled and our Yachats home and dozens of others received clear title. With our neighbors we began to heal emotionally from six years of fending off unprincipled litigation. In December Sarah received her diploma from GFU.

In May of 2003 Fern was hospitalized eleven days by an attack by a monstrous bug, "cloridium difficile," and on July 1 she played five holes of golf at Crestview and birdied number 7. Plucky gal! In July Arthur had two books published at the same time—*"Exploring Heaven"* (Harper), and *"Prayers at Twilight"* (Barclay Press).

Sister-in-law Lora Roberts died in August.

November 7, with family and friends, Fern and Arthur celebrated sixty years of marriage. God is good!

December 1, we moved to the Friendsview Retirement Community, Newberg, Oregon.

Articles, Lectures, Chapters, Honors, and Special Assignments

2015 Readings in *Fruit of the Vine,* a devotional quarterly; frequent contributions since the publication's founding in 1961 (see p. 142 sidebar)

2013 "Evangelical Friends" chapter in Quaker Studies, Oxford, ed. Angell and Dandelion

2012 Alumni lecture "Trouble and Triumph in Anthropolis"

2011 Commencement address "Truth and Love"

2009 *Reflections* (an internet column for NWYM pastors)

2007 "Good and Evil—A Paradigm" chapter *Quakers and Good and Evil,* ed. Dandelion (Ashgate)

2007 Foreword, *Holiness, the Soul of Quakerism,* by Carole Spencer (Paternoster)

2006 "Corresponding with George A. Fox" article in *Quaker History*

2006 Foreword, *To Be Silent...Would Be Criminal,* by Irv Brendlinger (Scarecrow)

2006 "Come In at the Door," chapter in *George Fox's Legacy, Friends for 350 Years* (Friends Historical Association)

2005 *Emmaus Road,* an Easter Cantata, music by David Howard (Pipermuse Press, 1994, rev. 2005)

2004 Introduction, *Quaker Theory,* ed. Ben Dandelion (Scarecrow)

2004 "Testimony" in *Walk Worthy of Your Calling,* ed. Abbott and Parsons (Friends United Press)

2003 *Historical Dictionary of Quakerism,* ed. Abbott et al. several articles (Scarecrow)

2002 "Come In at the Door! How Foxian Metaphors of Salvation Speak to Evangelical Friends," Swarthmore lecture, 350th Quaker Anniversary. Published in Friends History, 2004; book, 2006

1998 "Evangelical Perspective," *Friends and the Vietnam War* (Pendle Hill)

1998 "A Quaker Perspective," anthology, *Death and Afterlife* (Charles Press)

1997 Selected writings in *A Certain Kind of Perfection,*
ed. M. Post Abbott (Pendle Hill)

1994 "Jesus Is Lord" in *Practiced by the Light,*
ed. Snarr/Smith-Christopher (Friends United Press)

1992 "A Cherished Sentinel," poem in C.R. Hellen,
Alzheimer's Disease (Andover Medical)

1992 "John Frederick Hanson," in *The Lamb's War, Essays
in Honor of Hugh Barbour,* ed. Newman and Birkel,
(Earlham College Press)

1991 Malone College, "A New Call to Holiness,"
"Education as an Adventure in Hope"

1989 "Good and Evil in a Nuclear Age," Moscow, Russia,
(meeting cancelled, but paper shared with Institute
of Philosophy members)

1989-2000 Editor, *Quaker Religious
Thought*

1987 Chapter on Quakers, in
*Great Leaders of the Chris-
tian Church,* ed. Woodbridge
(Moody Press)

1987 *Faith and Practice,* Northwest Yearly Meeting, editor,
revised edition

1986 Teacher of the Year, George
Fox College

1986 Faculty Lecture, George Fox
College, "The Automobile as
Icon"

1986 "The Poet as Ombudsman for
the Universal," International
Philosophers for Prevention
of Nuclear Omnicide,
St. Louis

Quaker Religious Thought

Editor 1989-2000 and a
regular contributor. Topics
he addressed in *Quaker
Religious Thought* include:

Quaker Understanding
of Christ (1999)

Quakers and the Broader
Christian Movement (1996)

The Universalism of Christ in Early
Quaker Understanding (1989)

Holiness and Quaker Renewal
(1967)

Early Friends and the
Work of Christ (1961)

1984-87 "Ethics Across the Curriculum," Christian College
Consortium project

1984 Articles in *Evangelical Dictionary of Theology,*
ed. Elwell (Eerdmans)

1983 Articles in *Beacon Dictionary of Theology,*
ed. R. Taylor (Beacon Hill)

1981 "Eskimo Religion" chapter in *Canadian Journal of Native Studies,* 1 no. 1

1980 "The Quakers and the Eskimos," Address at the XIV Congress History of Religions (Winnipeg, Canada)

1980 Poetry in an anthology, *On the Edge of a Truth,* ed. Nancy Thomas (Barclay Press)

1980 Chapter in *Quaker Views on Eschatology,* ed. Dean Freiday (FWCC)

1980 Foreword, *Portrait of a Quaker, Levi T.Pennington,* by Donald McNichols (Barclay Press)

1977 Chapter, *Handbook of Church History,* ed. T. Downey (Lion/Eerdmans/Fortress) also 1990-95

1976 Chapter, *New Call to Peacemaking,* (Friends World Committee for Consultation)

1976 Chapter, *Friends in the Americas,* ed. Francis Hall (Friends World Committee for Consultation)

1974 Chapter, *Quaker Understanding of Christ and Authority* (Friends World Committee for Consultation)

1972-75 Charles Replogle Memorial Professor, George Fox College

1960, 1968, 1972 Guest instructor, Earlham School of Religion

1966 Chapter, *American Quakers Today,* ed. Ed Bronner (Friends world Committee for Consultation, rev. 1976)

1963-64 Alumnus of the Year, George Fox College

1960 Guest instructor, Malone College

1959-67 *Concern,* a magazine of the Association of Evangelical Friends, editor

1956 Faculty Lecturer, George Fox College, "Judgment and the Meaning of History"

1944-?? *Pacifica Theologica,* a ministry magazine, co-editor with Jack Willcuts

---

Fruit of the Vine
Daily devotionals by and for Friends

Founding editor with T. Eugene Coffin in 1961 and a regular contributor for fifty-five years.

Publications (author)

2015 *The Bonus Years*
a sequel to Drawn by the Light
(Barclay Press)

2009 *The County Road 804 Story*
[private publication]

2008 *Through Flaming Sword*
Life and Legacy of George Fox
50th anniversary revised edition
(Barclay Press)

2007 *Heavenly Fire*
a book of poems (Barclay Press)

2006 *The People Called Quakers*
pamphlet, 6th edition (Barclay Press)

2006 *The Sacred Ordinary:*
Sermons and Addresses (Barclay Press)

2006 *Messengers of God:*
the Sensuous Side of Spirituality,
rev. edition (Barclay Press)

2003 *Exploring Heaven*
(HarperSanFrancisco)

2003 *Prayers at Twilight*
(Barclay Press)

2001 *Robert Barclay's Catechism and Confession,*
ed. with Dean Freiday (Barclay Press)

2000 *Let the Spirit Soar*
mayoral poems
(City of Yachats/Barclay Press)

2000 *The Wit and Wisdom of Jack Willcuts*
(Barclay Press)

1997 *Look Closely at the Child*
Christmas poems (Barclay Press)

1996 *Messengers of God:*
the Sensuous Side of Spirituality
also revised edition 2006 (Barclay Press)

1994 *Soliloquy Syllabic*
Faculty Dialogue #23

1993 *Drawn by the Light:*
Autobiographical Reflections
(Barclay Press)

1990 *Back to Square One:*
Handling Losses, a series
of sermons (Barclay Press)

1988 *John Frederick Hanson*
a biographical study
(private printing); papers

1996 *Jonah ben Amittai,*
a musical (with Dave Miller)

1984 *Sunrise and Shadow,*
a book of poetry (Barclay Press)

1983 *Children of the Light,*
a musical (with Dave Miller)

1978 *Tomorrow Is Growing Old:*
Stories of Quakers in Alaska
(Barclay Press)

1977 *Alaska Quaker Documents,*
edited and microfilmed

1975 *History of the Association of Evangelical Friends*
(Barclay Press)

1974 *Listen to the Lord,*
a book of poetry (Barclay Press)

1973 *Early Quaker Writings*
ed. with Hugh Barbour
also reissued 2004(Eerdmans)

1967 *Move Over, Elijah,*
a book of poems and sermons
(Barclay Press)

1965 *Weeds among the Wheat*
Shrewsbury lecture pamphlet
(Woolman Press)

1959 *Through Flaming Sword*
a Spiritual Biography of George Fox
(Barclay Press)

Pastoral and Academic Ministry

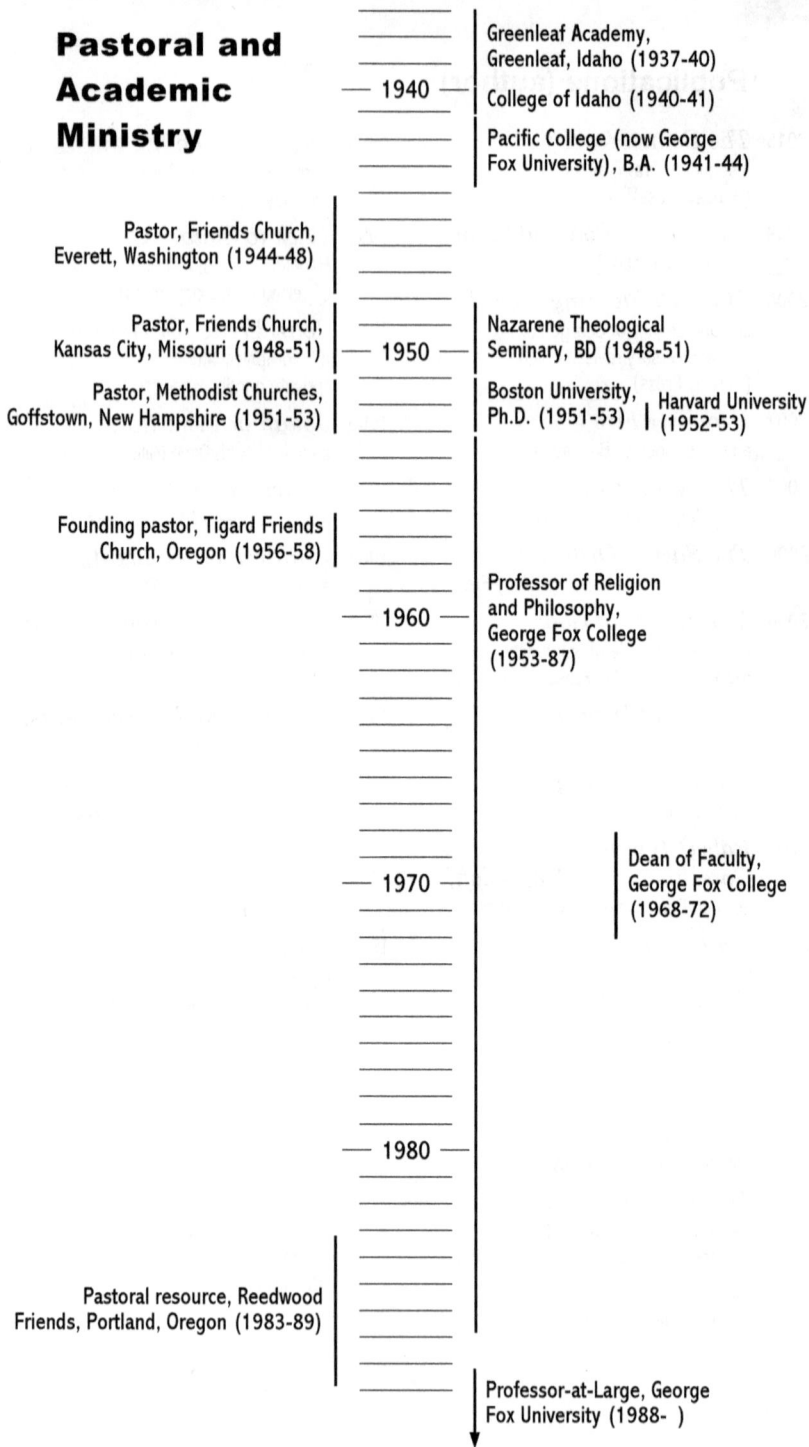

Greenleaf Academy, Greenleaf, Idaho (1937-40)

— 1940 —

College of Idaho (1940-41)

Pacific College (now George Fox University), B.A. (1941-44)

Pastor, Friends Church, Everett, Washington (1944-48)

Pastor, Friends Church, Kansas City, Missouri (1948-51)

— 1950 —

Nazarene Theological Seminary, BD (1948-51)

Pastor, Methodist Churches, Goffstown, New Hampshire (1951-53)

Boston University, Ph.D. (1951-53) | Harvard University (1952-53)

Founding pastor, Tigard Friends Church, Oregon (1956-58)

Professor of Religion and Philosophy, George Fox College (1953-87)

— 1960 —

— 1970 —

Dean of Faculty, George Fox College (1968-72)

— 1980 —

Pastoral resource, Reedwood Friends, Portland, Oregon (1983-89)

Professor-at-Large, George Fox University (1988-)

144

www.ingramcontent.com/pod-product-compliance
Lightning Source LLC
Chambersburg PA
CBHW051841090426
42736CB00011B/1920